Risk Modeling

Wiley and SAS Business Series

The Wiley and SAS Business Series presents books that help senior level managers with their critical management decisions.

Titles in the Wiley and SAS Business Series include:

For more information on any of the above titles, please visit www.wiley.com.

Risk Modeling

Practical Applications of Artificial Intelligence, Machine Learning, and Deep Learning

Terisa Roberts

Stephen J. Tonna

WILEY

Published by John Wiley & Sons, Inc., Hoboken, New Jersey.
Published simultaneously in Canada.

For general information on our other products and services or for technical support, please contact our Customer Care Department within the United States at (800) 762-2974, outside the United States at (317) 572-3993 or fax (317) 572-4002.

Wiley also publishes its books in a variety of electronic formats. Some content that appears in print may not be available in electronic formats. For more information about Wiley products, visit our web site at www.wiley.com.

Library of Congress Cataloging-in-Publication Data is Available:

ISBN 9781119824930 (Hardback)
ISBN 9781119824954 (ePDF)
ISBN 9781119824947 (epub)

Cover Design: Wiley
Cover Image: © Berkah/Getty Images

SKY10035642_080822

Contents

Acknowledgments

Terisa Roberts: To my husband, best friend, and partner, Johan, and our three children, Gary, Cara, and Isabella. Thank you for making me laugh. Stay curious and always keep dreaming.

Stephen J. Tonna: To my darling wife, Nini, and newborn son, Sebastian James, who have both heard the "tap" of laptop keys into the early mornings . . . my apologies for all the noise, but the amazing outcome is that little Sebastian is now an avid fan of both typing on laptop to help Papa and learning principles of machine learning algorithms!

Preface

FUTURE OF RISK MODELING

It is said that we are entering the fifth industrial revolution: the age of artificial intelligence. The ability of computers to start performing human tasks (called artificial intelligence, AI) and the wider use of complex algorithms that detect nonlinear relationships and self-learn (called machine learning) are starting to mature from experimentation to production and, in turn, revolutionizing many aspects of the financial services industry.

The uptake of these technologies for process automation and in digital customer journeys is growing exponentially in many industries, yet we are observing a more conservative and slower uptake in financial risk management. In an era where so much information is available on the use of AI and machine learning, financial organizations are cautious about its pertinence in regulated areas that expect compliance and transparency in decision-making.

At the same time, the digital revolution is occurring against a backdrop of an increasingly uncertain world. Volatility is at an all-time high. The risk management function is contending with new types of risks every day. Organizations around the world are dealing with myriad risks such as a haphazard recovery from the COVID-19 pandemic, rising inflation, cumulating geopolitical risks, and the impacts of climate change.

With this book, we want to highlight the strengths and weaknesses of AI and machine learning and explain how both can be effectively applied to everyday risk management problems, as well as efficiently evaluating the impacts of shocks under uncertainty, such as global pandemics and changes in the climate. Throughout the text, we aim to clarify misconceptions about the use of AI and machine learning using clear explanations, while offering practical advice for implementing the technologies into an organization's risk management framework.

With the right controls, AI and machine learning can deliver tangible benefits and become useful tools in the toolkit of the risk function. It can improve the accuracy and speed of risk assessments compared to human-led or other traditional methods of decision-making, and at the same time introduce new ways of work in risk management through increased automation. The rewards for innovation are not without risks of their own, and these technologies are largely under-regulated today (although, that will change in the future). In this book, we also highlight the barriers that organizations face in using AI and machine learning and provide ways to overcome them.

The book is structured to introduce AI and machine learning in the context of financial risk modeling, including the onboarding and preparation of diverse datasets. Throughout the book, we provide real-world risk management applications. The book contains dedicated material on model implementation, explainability, and addressing bias and fairness. It also provides details on extending model governance frameworks to AI and machine learning, the use of optimization in machine learning, and how AI and machine learning can help risk managers better assess and address new types of risks like climate change.

With the transformational advances in AI and machine learning, together with the radical speed of new development, as an industry, we are only scratching the surface in its practical application in financial risk management. With this book we aim to enable organizations to continue putting in place the right frameworks and infrastructure to enable modern technologies, and more importantly, build proficiency and capacity in AI and machine learning.

Risk Modeling

CHAPTER **1**

Introduction

"By far, the greatest danger of Artificial Intelligence is that people conclude too early that they understand it."

—Eliezer Yudkowsky

No doubt, we, as a society, are entering into new advances in technology at ground-breaking speed. The rapid growth in digital data and advances in computing power open endless possibilities for transformation in every sphere of life. At the same time, these developments are also driving unparalleled change in human behavior, consumer demand, and expectations. It is believed that we are now entering the next wave of revolution: the fifth industrial revolution or the age of artificial intelligence (AI). In this age, it is said that machines are truly capable of varying degrees of self-determination, reason, and "thought," working with humans in unison. As a technology, AI is pervasive in every industry, including financial services. It is also starting to mature as a useful tool in risk management function.

However, *AI* is a broad term and defined by various industry bodies in different ways. The *Oxford Dictionary* defines it as "the theory and development of computer systems able to perform tasks normally requiring human intelligence, such as visual perception, speech recognition, decision-making, and translation between languages."[1] The European Union defines it as "systems that display intelligent behaviour by analysing their environment and taking actions—with some degree of autonomy—to achieve specific goals."[2] The Office of the Comptroller of the Currency (OCC) in the United States defines it as "the application of computational tools to address tasks traditionally requiring human analysis."[3]

As a scientific discipline, AI includes several subdisciplines, such as machine learning (of which deep learning and reinforcement learning are examples), machine reasoning (which includes knowledge representation, deduction, and induction), and robotics (which includes sensors and the integration of other techniques into cyberphysical systems). Despite the enormous transformational benefits that true "AI" systems and platforms can bring to humanity, what is it about "AI" that sends shivers down our spines? Arguably, the shivers are caused by the fact that, for the first time in human history, we are engaging with the *intelligence* component of technology and the fear of the unknown. And another reason is Hollywood!

It is quite amazing that one of the most memorable moments in cinema is from Stanley Kubrick's 1968 production of Arthur C. Clarke's *2001: A Space Odyssey*.[4] In an iconic scene, the heuristically programmed algorithmic computer (HAL), responsible for controlling the systems of the *Discovery One* spacecraft, replies to astronaut David Bowman's request, "Open the pod bay doors, HAL," with *"I'm sorry, Dave. I'm afraid I can't do that."* Perhaps this scene is so memorable, because it is unbelievable to think that an advanced, sentient machine like HAL can think, feel, and mimic human behavior and decide on its own.

There are scenes from other movies and science fiction novels that depict AI as ultimately rising and taking control of society. In many ways, AI-enabled systems are already safely integrated into our personal lives. Take, for example, virtual assistants like Google Assistant, Apple's Siri, and Amazon's Alexa that use the more traditionally derived and AI-puritan List Processing (LISP) for voice recognition. Such "AI" has been widely adopted[5] and will continue its advancements as more applications integrate AI methodologies. This is true for the traditional AI applications like machine learning and deep learning to computer vision and cognitive computing as employed by next-generation televisions, cars, and home appliances.[6] In addition, technologies or machines utilizing AI or developed using machine or deep learning algorithms (concepts we will cover in Chapter 3) have contributed to the advancement of robotic process automation (RPA), which refers to the automation of repeatable processes by computer-coded software programs that were traditionally done by humans. One of the reasons why RPA is starting to replace other, more traditional operational efficiency improvement strategies is because it runs at a fraction of the cost of human capital.[7] In addition to the cost-savings, RPA has reduced processing time and error rates. Examples of RPA deployments in banks include virtual assistants that handle repetitive tasks such as document-processing and verification, account opening and funds transfers, and correction of formatting and data errors that arise in customer requests.

By continuing to augment, and at times automate, manual jobs or daily tasks, AI-enabled applications continue to transform our personal and professional lives. AI is making what was once science-fiction into science-fact. This will continue to be the case when considering the consolidated impact of four major factors:[8]

- **Moore's law.** Computing power is said to double every two years and will continue to do so for the foreseeable future.[9]

- **Data.** The creation of data and replication have doubled each year. It is estimated that 1.7 megabytes of new information are created every second for every human being on the planet, meaning that from 2010 to 2020, there was a 5,000% growth in data—from 1.2 trillion gigabytes in 2010 to 59 trillion gigabytes in 2020. The exponential growth in data is largely driven by digitalization, and is expected to continue.[10] It is the fuel for AI-based algorithms, especially those that require large and rich amounts of data for training and development, like deep learning.[11]

- **Funding.** AI funding has doubled every two years, largely driven by the availability of required computational power.[12]

- **Test of time.** There is 50 years of established AI and quantitative research that is underpinning better algorithms.

Taking these four factors into account and the current state of play, AI is not merely hype. Although we are going through a hype cycle where expectations may not be realistic, there is great potential that will likely be realized in the coming years.[13] To remain relevant in the wake of the age of AI, it is critical for organizations to prepare for a large-scale adoption, integration, and use of AI-enabled systems in industries such as financial services. A word of caution, though—for AI and machine learning to realize short- and long-term business value in a responsible way, the foundational technological building blocks of data, people, and processes will need to be reconsidered. These building blocks will be discussed in more detail throughout this book.

RISK MODELING: DEFINITION AND BRIEF HISTORY

In recent years, the number of risk models employed by financial institutions increased dramatically, by 10–25% annually.[14] Let's define what a risk model is. A risk model involves the application of quantitative methods, analytics, and algorithms to quantify financial and nonfinancial risks. It is important to note that risk management applies to other industries besides financial institutions; however, the applications used in this book mainly relate to the financial services industry and particularly to the quantification of financial risks.

Henceforth, in this book, the term model refers to a financial risk model unless otherwise stated. Interestingly, most of the modern-day risk and probability theory evolved from innovation in science, economics, and technology in the last 200 to 300 years.[15] However, our ability to utilize mathematics to estimate probabilities and use it as a means to quantify risk in our modern world stems from developmental advances across multiple centuries. The English term *hazard*, referring to "chance of loss or harm, risk," likely originates from the Arabic term *az-zahr*, which means "the dice." Ground-breaking mathematicians like Fibonacci (the golden ratio), followed by Blaise Pascal (the father of modern theory in decision-making), laid the foundations for modern-day probability theory.

Moreover, Fibonacci learned the Hindu-Arabic numerical system from traders while visiting his father at a port in Algeria in the thirteenth century. Innovations in mathematics, trading, and finance seem inextricably linked—but that is perhaps a topic for another book. The use of risk models can likely be traced back to the precursor of what we now consider actuarial science in insurance. In the eighteenth century, these pre-modern-day analysts poured over data to estimate life expectancy on which to price insurance premiums.

Fast forward to modern times; based on the work of others like David Hume and Nicholas Bernoulli, Harry Markowitz developed portfolio theory in 1952. Today, we can define a model as a quantitative method, system, or approach that applies statistical, economic, financial, or mathematical theories, techniques, and assumptions to process input data into quantitative estimates.[16]

The use of risk models is now ubiquitous in financial services. One reason is the swaths of new regulations before and after the Global Financial Crisis. In the last decade, regulation after new regulation has expanded the volume of risk models that organizations need to manage. In addition, organizations have increased model usage to remain competitive—replacing manual activities and decision-making with analytical methods, while improving the sophistication of their models. Models are also used to keep up with industry trends such as big data and digitalization.

The effects of the Global Financial Crisis did not only increase the number of models to manage—it also increased their complexity. Organizations began adding different model types—including econometric models, financial and forward-looking models for provisioning, and enterprise stress testing. That resulted in a growing number of dependencies and interconnections between the models, how they operate, and the process that defines it (i.e., the risk model lifecycle).

New models have started to gain even more traction as the COVID-19 pandemic highlighted inefficiencies in the risk model lifecycle. The issues were particularly evident in the volatility observed in forward-looking loss models during the COVID-19 pandemic. Financial institutions realized that risk models need to balance their efficacy with potentially longer-term degraded conditions and increased macroeconomic uncertainty, caused by the COVID-19 pandemic. The longer-term conditions and increased uncertainty are likely to continue to create "shocks" to many different types of risk models. At the time of writing, many large banks have accelerated their recalibration efforts, including the use of alternative data and modeling approaches, due to:

- Risk-ranking and risk profiling discrepancies caused by shifts in consumer and portfolio behavior
- Risk models simply breaking down due to shifts in correlations with macroeconomic indicators

The use of AI and machine-learning-based algorithms for risk management requires a rethink of the risk model lifecycle. Typically, a traditional statistical model takes a risk modeling team several months of development effort. One can argue that a lengthy process is needed to ensure a desired level of accuracy, performance, and validation, but experience has shown that a lot of effort is spent on inefficiencies due to fragmented, legacy systems across the risk model lifecycle. For example, rigid processes that are entrenched in silos of business activity may delay signoffs and there can be a culture that supports a mentality to "reinvent the wheel" for each model development activity.

One lesson from COVID-19 is that long cycles of building and deploying models for risk-based decision-making lead to suboptimal decisions.

The use of AI and machine learning presents an opportunity to greatly reduce the "time to model" and reap the resulting rewards.

USE OF AI AND MACHINE LEARNING IN RISK MODELING

As a suite of tools, AI and machine learning have transformational potential to improve accuracy compared to traditional models, handle large structured and unstructured datasets, and help assist organizations with agile responses to changes in market conditions. Together, the suite has been effectively used in problem-solving, and is likely to accelerate given the faster adoption of big data technologies and digitalization.

In financial services, the use of AI and machine learning started some years prior to the COVID-19 outbreak and in many diverse areas of financial services, including risk management. To the risk function, AI and machine learning have delivered tangible benefits by automating mundane tasks and processing large volumes of diverse data. These tools can flexibly identify complex relationships hidden in data and thus achieve higher levels of model accuracy, compared to what is possible with traditional statistical methods. However, for the large-scale and long-term use of AI and machine learning, adoption of a scientific mindset needs to be better embedded in the culture and in the way innovation is approached by teams across the enterprise.

When applying the scientific mindset to AI and machine learning, technology is typically applied to solving a specific problem, rather than attempting to use the technology to *incidentally* solve an existing problem. Once a problem has been identified, then a hypothesis can be tested appropriately, utilizing the scientific fundamentals that involve data, people, and processes. We will next explain how the traditional function of risk management is changing in response to new and emerging risks, and how AI and machine learning can enable an easier response to the demands created.

THE NEW RISK MANAGEMENT FUNCTION

Risk management can be viewed as more than a collection of compliance measures and a function to meet continued demands and expectations of internal and external governance bodies. Current risk management frameworks are adapting to new and emerging risks, increased uncertainty in the macroeconomic environment, and addressing transparency and fairness in financial decision-making—especially those concerning customers and those that impact the environment. Emerging risks, digitalization, stronger competition, and new regulations demand more from the modern risk function, especially against a backdrop of COVID-19 and climate change.

At the time of writing, a tiny, single-stranded RNA called severe acute respiratory syndrome coronavirus 2 (SARS-CoV-2) that causes Coronavirus Disease-2019 (COVID-19) and potential life-threatening respiratory infections, had quickly spread to become a global pandemic.[17] Beginning about December 2019, the impact and devastation caused by that tiny strand of RNA was unprecedented in contemporary times. The impact of lockdowns on the global economy was sharp and steep: the worldwide unemployment rate peaked at 14.5% in April 2020[18] with a worldwide gross domestic product (GDP) contraction of at least 5.2%.[19] All economic factors pointed to one of the worst economic crises the world had experienced since the 1930s Great Depression.

Part of the dramatic volatility caused by containment measures were fortunately countered by fiscal policy, including short-term relief for borrowers and other programs introduced by national governments and central banks. Irrespective of the extent of containment measures, the resiliency built into banks' balance sheets—large capital buffers put in place as a result of enhanced regulatory scrutiny following the Global Financial Crisis[20]—were tested by the pandemic.

Who would have thought that a tiny strand of RNA could create such macroeconomic upheaval in as little as a few months? Many businesses had to adapt to a newly defined "normal."

Even though the impacts of the pandemic were quick and severe, the recovery was almost as quick, as countries and sovereign states emerged from the COVID-19 restrictions and trillions of dollars in stimulus measures boosted economies.

The macroeconomic effects at the peak of the pandemic created strong negative impacts on risk and profitability levels of organizations and demanded quick intervention from governments. For financial services, for example, risk and profitability are known to interact very closely with macroeconomic effects (as per the credit cycle or interest rate cycle). In addition, financial services play a necessary and important part in stabilizing markets for businesses to operate.[21] Such macroeconomic factors, continued uncertainty, and market responses may drive unexpected impacts on all types of financial risk, including credit, market, and liquidity risk.

The main types of financial and nonfinancial risks are summarized in Table 1.1.

Changes to the climate have been understood for many decades. Since 1992, the United Nations has recognized that changes to the global climate patterns, mostly due to greenhouse gas emissions, pose serious issues to the world.[22] The recognition has created notable accords by participating countries. However, more recently, data and scientific-based analysis suggest that more needs to be done sooner. We are at a crossroads of climate instability. Climate change, defined as "a significant variation of average weather conditions" (i.e., the increased likelihood of warmer, wetter, or drier climate conditions over the next several decades)[23] will start to have significant economic

Table 1.1 Types of Risk and Associated Definitions

Risk Type	Definition
Credit risk	Risk of financial loss due to a borrower's failure to repay loan obligations.
Market risk	Risk of loss to institutions earnings from movement in market prices.
Operational risk	Risk of loss from a failed internal process, people, system, or external event.
Insurance risk	Harmful or unexpected event, threat, or peril for which insurance is provided.
Liquidity risk	Risk arising from a firm's inability to meet its short-term obligations as they become due.
Reputation risk	Risk of financial and nonfinancial loss due to public opinion.
Strategic risk	Risk from adverse business decisions or lack of responsiveness to changes in the industry and operating environment.
Compliance risk	Risk from violations of laws or regulations, internal policies and procedures, or ethical standards.
Interest rate risk	Risk of loss due to movements in interest rates.

and socioeconomic impacts under different warming scenarios from now until 2100.

The stability of the climate and financial services industry is intricately connected by complex layers of interaction between the macroeconomic, financial, and climate systems.[24] Stability can be best addressed by understanding what the climate change–associated risks are to the finance sector. We discuss these along with addressing the analytics framework, covering data, models, and scenarios that are needed to understand the impacts of climate change in Chapter 9. Importantly, climatic change is an area where advanced analytics and innovative applications of AI and machine learning have added value.

OVERCOMING BARRIERS TO TECHNOLOGY AND AI ADOPTION WITH A LITTLE HELP FROM NATURE

At this point you may be asking yourself, is it purely that we are waiting for true "AI" to be created before it becomes mainstream in its use, or are other factors at play acting as barriers of uptake? One way to narrow down the naturally derived barriers of larger-scale adoption of new technologies is to look back in time at periods of industrial revolutions.

When a new technological advancement like means of communication and societal systems synergize, it has created industrial revolutions that in turn have acted to modernize society through innovation.[25] Quite paradoxically, in practice, the ensuing new ways of working and organizational change required have been less glamorous, and often challenging. There are many such examples of innovative techniques and associated technologies where genuine concerns were held that prolonged the required change and delayed adoption at scale. Take, for example, the first industrial age during the eighteenth century, where the change of wood power to coal power led to the replacement of hand tools with power-driven machines like the steam engine.[26] The second industrial age saw the use of electric power for mass production and rapid standardization. Yet the humble telephone was believed to cause deafness or simply send people mad.[27] Fast forward to the third industrial revolution that began in the 1950s to 1970s, where technology advanced from analogue electronic and mechanical devices to electronic computing, digital record-keeping, and the advent of the internet. Yet the first version of the automated teller machine (ATM) called the "Banko graph" was met with concern that customers would lose all their money! Customers were promised that the machines were safe and convenient, allowing them to make deposits or withdraw cash at any hour of the day or night.[28] Photographs of money entering the machine as a form of direct receipt[29] were not enough to allay fears. It took the semi-catastrophic weather event of the 1977 blizzard in New York that caused mass bank closures for many days for ATM usage to become more widespread.[30] The rest, with no intentional pun, is history, as other cities around the world followed New York's lead.[31]

A little push to drive change like the ATM, coupled with a climate event, is at times needed to accelerate the adoption of technological innovation. However repetitive and mundane, transformation is not easy and requires hard work. For organic innovation to progress, technological changes like the ATM and even telephone often require experience through experimentation rather than mandates so that the needs and necessities of change, as well as its opportunities and risks, can be fully understood. With that in mind, eventual desire for change can even be created.[32]

Similarly, the mainstream adoption of AI and machine learning in risk modeling requires both experimentation and experience to be fully understood. As suggested by the ATM example, while adoption of new technology may, at times, require a shock, broad adoption occurs when the technology improves the customer experience. If that does not take place, then the tangible benefits of AI and machine learning may not be fully leveraged.

THIS BOOK: WHAT IT IS AND IS NOT

With this book, we aim to provide examples and information to demystify the concepts of AI and machine learning, thereby increasing the awareness of its many benefits and how it can be applied to solve everyday risk management problems (e.g., how to evaluate the financial impact of extreme events such as global pandemics and changes in climate). We also highlight some of the incremental risks and unintended consequences associated with AI and machine learning in risk management and ways to address these, thereby enabling organizations to be better prepared for its adoption and responsible use. As far as possible, we aim to provide practical examples of use cases where AI and machine learning have delivered tangible benefits in risk management.

ENDNOTES

1. Oxford Reference, *The Oxford Dictionary of Phrase and Fable* (2006), https://www.oxfordreference.com/view/10.1093/oi/authority.20110803095426960

2. The European Commission's High Level Expert Group on Artificial Intelligence, *A Definition of AI: Main Capabilities and Scientific Disciplines* (European Commission, 2018).

3. Office of the Comptroller of the Currency, *Comptroller's Handbook: Safety and Soundness. Model Risk Management Version 1* (Federal Reserve Bank, 2021), https://www.occ.gov/publications-and-resources/publications/comptrollers-handbook/files/model-risk-management/pub-ch-model-risk.pdf

4. Grant Feller, *Future Technology: A Force for Good or a Source of Fear?* (Coventry, UK: The University of Warwick, 2015).

5. Anand S. Rao, Gerard Verweij, and E. Cameron, *Sizing the Prize—What's the Real Value of AI for Your Business and How Can You Capitalise?* (Boston: Pricewaterhouse-Coopers, 2017).

6. Margot O'Neill, *Explainer: What is artificial intelligence?* (Melbourne, Australia: ABC News, 2017); Rao et al., *Sizing the Prize.*

7. Shane O'Sullivan and Brandon Stafford, *RPA and Your Digitisation Strategy* (Australia: PricewaterhouseCoopers (Australia) Pty Ltd., 2016).

8. Tara Balakrishnan, Michael Chui, Bryce Hall, and Nicolaus Henke, *The state of AI in 2020* (London: McKinsey & Company, 2020), https://www.mckinsey.com/business-functions/quantumblack/our-insights/global-survey-the-state-of-ai-in-2020

9. Dave Vellante and David Floyer, "A new era of innovation: Moore's Law is not dead and AI is ready to explode," *SiliconAngle* (April 20, 2021), https://siliconangle.com/2021/04/10/new-era-innovation-moores-law-not-dead-ai-ready-explode/

10. Gil Press, "54 Predictions about the state of data in 2021," *Forbes* (December 30, 2020), https://www.forbes.com/sites/gilpress/2020/12/30/54-predictions-about-the-state-of-data-in-2021/?sh=30985b47397d

11. Joe McKendrick, "AI adoption skyrocketed over the last 18 months," *Harvard Business Review* (Sept 27, 2021), https://hbr.org/2021/09/ai-adoption-skyrocketed-over-the-last-18-months

12. PricewaterhouseCoopers, *UK Economic Outlook: Propsects for the Housing Market and the Impact of AI on Jobs* (United Kingdom: PricewaterhouseCoopers, July 2018), https://www.pwc.co.uk/services/economics/insights/uk-economic-outlook/july-18.html

13. PricewaterhouseCoopers, *UK Economic Outlook.*

14. Ignacio Crespo, Pankaj Kumar, Peter Noteboom, and Marc Taymans, *The Evolution of Model Risk Management* (New York: McKinsey & Company, 2017), http://dln.jaipuria.ac.in:8080/jspui/bitstream/123456789/3127/1/The-evolution-of-model-risk-management.pdf

15. Philip F. Stahel, Ivor S. Douglas, Todd F. VanderHeiden, and Sebastian Weckbach, "The history of risk: a revie," *World Journal of Emergency Surgery* (March 14, 2017).

16. Federal Reserve Bank, *SR11/7—Supervisory Guidance on Model Risk Management* (Washington DC: Board of Governors of the Federal Reserve System and Office of the Comptroller of the Currency, 2011), https://www.federalreserve.gov/supervisionreg/srletters/sr1107.htm

17. Center for Systems Science and Engineering (CSSE) at Johns Hopkins University (JHU), *COVID-19 Dashboard* (2020), https://coronavirus.jhu.edu/map.html

18. OECD, *Unemployment Rate—Tackling coronavirus (Covid19)*, Château de la Muette (Paris, France: OECD, 2020).

19. The World Bank, *The Global Economic Outlook During the COVID-19 Pandemic: A Changed World* (Washington, DC: The World Bank, 2020).

20. Fabio Natalucci, *Global Financial Stability Amid Covid-19 Pandemic* [Interview] (April 2, 2020).

21. Marianne Gizycki, *The Effect of Macroeconomic Conditions on Bank's Risk and Profitability* (Melbourne, AUS: Reserve Bank of Australia, 2001).

22. United Nations, *UN Climate Talks 1992–2020* (New York: The United Nations, 2020).

23. Melissa Denchak, *Global Climate Change: What You Need to Know* (New York: NRDC, 2017).

24. Network for Greening the Financial System, *NGFS—Central Banks and Supervisors Network for Greening the Financial System* (Accessed 2021), https://www.ngfs.net/en

25. Joseph A. Schumpeter, *Business Cycles: A Theoretical, Historical and Statistical Analysis of the Capitalist Process* (New York and London: McGraw Hill Book Company Inc., 1939); Goncalo de Vasconcelos, "The Third Industrial Revolution—Internet, Energy and a New Financial System," *Forbes* (March 4, 2015).

26. Punit Renjen, *Industry 4.0: Are you ready?* (Philadelphia, PA: Deloitte Review, 2018), https://www2.deloitte.com/content/dam/insights/us/articles/4364_Industry4-0_Are-you-ready/4364_Industry4-0_Are-you-ready_Report.pdf; Peter Temin, "Two views of the British Industrial Revolution," *Journal of Economic History* 57(1) (1997): 63–82.

27. Natasha Lomas, *Humanity has Always Feared Technology. In the 21st Century, Are We Right to Be Afraid?* (Palo Alto, CA: ZD Net.com, 2011); Melissa Dickson, *The Victorians Had the Same Concerns about Technology as We Do* (Oxford, UK: The Conversation, 2016).

28. Elizabeth S. Anderson, *10 Unnecessary Fears People Had of Everyday Things* (UK: Listverse Pty Ltd., 2015); History.com, *Automated Teller Machines* (A&E Television Networks, 2010; updated 2018), https://www.history.com/topics/inventions/automated-teller-machines; Cornelis Robat, *ATM—Automatic Teller Machine* (2006), thocp.net

29. Elizabeth S. Anderson, *10 Unnecessary Fears People Had of Everyday Things* (UK: Listverse Pty Ltd., 2015).

30. History.com, *Automated Teller Machines*.

31. Robat, *ATM*.

32. Richard Beckhard and Reuben T. Harris, *Organizational Transitions: Managing Complex Change*, 2nd ed. (Reading, MA: Addison-Wesley, 1987); John Kotter, *Leading Change*, 1st ed. (Boston, MA: Harvard Business School Press, 1996).

CHAPTER 2

Data Management and Preparation

"Deep learning craves big data because big data is necessary to isolate hidden patterns and to find answers without over-fitting the data. With deep learning, the better-quality data you have, the better the results."

—Wayne Thompson, SAS Chief Data Scientist

Data has become a vital resource for organizations, entities, and governments alike.

For the risk management function, data has always been a pivotal enabler. Since its inception as a scientific discipline, sound risk management has been underpinned by efficiency in obtaining and retrieving of information—at the time when it's needed—and robust data management. To name a few examples, data is used to inform risk assessments, monitor risks, and help to detect new types of risks. For risk modeling, real-time and granular data are increasingly being used to develop, monitor, and maintain better and more innovative risk models.

A critical lesson learned from the Global Financial Crisis was that banks' information technology (IT) and data architectures were inadequate to support the broad management of financial risks. Some banks were unable to manage their risks properly because of weak risk data aggregation capabilities and risk-reporting practices. This had severe consequences for the banks themselves and to the stability of the financial system. In response, the Basel Committee on Banking Standards (BCBS) developed a standard with principles for effective risk data, its aggregation, and final reporting under standard number 239.

In recent years, digitalization and the digital footprints left by consumers and businesses have caused a rapid growth in data sources available for analysis, broadening the possibilities to generate insights beyond those from traditional data sources. Today, the risk function is operating in a world with increasing demand for better digital services and data-driven decision-making. Other initiatives like open banking (or consent-based data exchange), the availability of a plethora of proprietary and open-source tools, and cloud computing have a significant impact on value creation in financial services. With the growth of these initiatives and the mainstream use of advanced analytics and machine learning, these innovations require strong data foundations.

Notwithstanding the benefits of having more data, it also presents an increased number of challenges, including access to good-quality data, cybersecurity, and the responsible use of personal data. Robust data management is critical for the adoption of artificial intelligence (AI) and machine learning as the modeling approaches become much more data driven. AI and machine learning can identify and explore subtleties in big data and can better handle "alternative data."

The term *big data* refers to data that is so large, fast, or complex that it is difficult or impossible to process using traditional methods.

The concept of big data gained momentum when industry analyst Doug Laney articulated its definition using three *V*s:

1. **Volume.** Organizations collect data from a variety of sources, including business transactions, third-party data providers, news articles, and more. In the past, storing it would have been a problem, but more economical storage on cloud-based platforms and data lakes has eased the burden.

2. **Velocity.** With the growth in real-time data, data streams into businesses at an ever-increasing speed and must be handled in a timely manner.

3. **Variety.** Using larger data means that diverse types of data must be leveraged that is not necessarily structured as dimensional tables. Unstructured data sources such as sensor data, images, and social media updates add to the variety of data.

Looking ahead, the expectations from regulators are clear: risk calculations will need to be performed at much higher levels of granularity, with greater emphasis on the use of high-quality data, especially when advanced algorithms are being used for risk model development.

The risks of incorporating these emerging data sources in risk management, such as "alternative data," are that these may violate consumer protection and fair lending laws. That may lead to unintended consequences in the use of AI and machine learning. The unintended consequences of AI and machine learning are often amplified, as the lack of explainability of the AI and machine learning masks the underlying data issues. The abstraction hidden in the layers of a deep learning algorithm is where existing approaches for data quality may fall short: organizations may have to turn to AI to manage the risks in the data.

The use of AI and machine learning cannot function outside existing business processes. For organizations to benefit from its use, a comprehensive approach to enterprise data management is required, spanning across the silos of data collection, modeling, downstream processes, reporting, and disclosures. In essence, for AI and machine learning, the governance of data becomes as important as the governance of the models.

IMPORTANCE OF DATA GOVERNANCE TO THE RISK FUNCTION

Historically, many organizations have lacked a strategic approach to data management and preparation. For financial institutions, compliance with the BCBS239 principles meant that organizations had to fortify their data aggregation and reporting capability by tracking the accuracy, integrity, and completeness of the data used for risk measurement and management.

The BCBS239 guidance represented a major transformational challenge for financial institutions around the globe since its development in the wake of the Global Financial Crisis. The BCBS239 guidance has four very closely related topics that help with better and more uniform risk exposure management:

1. Risk governance and infrastructure
2. Risk data aggregation
3. Risk reporting practices
4. Risk supervisory review

These four topics are supported by 11 principles, as shown in Figure 2.1. Several of these principles focus on improving data quality and data management to help with better and more uniform risk exposure management.

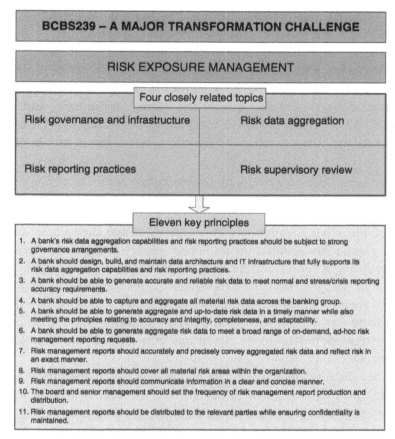

Figure 2.1 The framework of the Basel Banking Standards (BCBS) standard number 239. The BCBS239 has represented a major transformational challenge for banks around the globe since its development in the wake of the Global Financial Crisis.

Other regulations, such as GDPR (Global Data Protection Regulation) and open banking, also require financial institutions to strengthen data governance.

Regardless of regulatory expectations, strong data management practices are a competitive advantage for data-driven decision-making. For good-quality models and decisions, good-quality data is a prerogative.

As a first step, organizations need to establish an enterprise data governance framework. This will then be supplemented by sound data integration and data preparation practices.

However, without the fundamentals of data preparation and its management in place—that includes the use of data dictionaries, standardized datasets, and data quality and validation routines—adhering to BCBS239 (Figure 2.1) will continue to be a challenge for many financial institutions, and many are still in the process of full adoption.

FUNDAMENTALS OF DATA MANAGEMENT

Many tools can be used to explore data and prepare it for risk modeling, but what is commonly encountered is that the sample design and approaches adopted for traditional models are often considered enough for AI and machine learning to be applied with rigor. This assumes that the fundamentals of data preparation and its management are present within the financial institution. Unfortunately, these fundamentals are not always in place to a meaningful degree, especially to support data-driven algorithms, even 14 years after the Global Financial Crisis.

For the fundamentals of data preparation and management to be more easily achieved and to ensure that the data is fit-for-purpose to leverage advanced algorithms, an enterprise data strategy that will support best practices for AI and machine learning is needed. Let us look at each of the fundamental topics. In addition, AI and machine learning can be used to achieve these objectives more easily.

Master Data Management

Organizations have access to copious amounts of internal and external data. However, one of the largest gaps faced by financial institutions large and small is the key concept of data catalogs. Many institutions attempt to fill this gap with spreadsheet-based descriptions of datasets that quickly become outdated as new columns or rows are added, like new financial products. Automation enabled by AI and machine learning can help build data catalogs that include the ability to easily search for data and shared columns or observations across datasets. The search queries utilize natural language processing to improve ease of use. Organizations can build custom solutions using a programmatic approach or utilize vendor-provided applications with built-in AI technologies.

For example, a standard data catalog provides the following basic metadata for each dataset:

- Column details
- Row details
- Size of the data
- Completeness of the data (i.e., number of "missing" fields)
- How the data is accessed and where it is located
- Data security
- Purpose of the data (this can be manually added or automated)
- Data lineage and history of usage (i.e., how many reports, models, and jobs have been completed using the data, and the main users of the table)

Standardizing Datasets and Ensuring Data Quality

For AI and machine learning, risk management teams may decide that all the data profiling metrics generated today are enough.

We recall a very profound statement made by a prolific professor at a conference when challenged about the output results of a model: "*Well, the data is the data!*" This can be true. Data that is sourced and used in a risk model is "the data," but importantly, it can be improved and cleansed using sophisticated cognitive data-quality controls. These measures ascertain the data with regards to its uniqueness and descriptive statistics such as average values and mean, median, mode, and standard deviation. When more sophisticated and repeatable techniques are used, that "little bit of guesswork" is removed and the data cleansing becomes less manual.

In practical terms, the data catalog information can be extended further, by descriptive data quality metrics and whether the data matches the expected distributions (e.g., if the catalog expects integer data but it is a string, then it will be recorded as a mismatch). Data-quality metrics are also extremely useful to provide details on the completeness of the dataset. These include, but are not limited to:

- Frequency of uniqueness, missing values, number of mismatches
- Metadata measures that provide information on columns, including its type, format, length, and candidates for primary keys
- Security scores that will automatically detect columns that contain personally identifiable or sensitive information
- Semantic types by combining data-quality algorithms and natural language processing to automatically generate metadata (e.g., the columns representing numeric values, identification numbers, and postcodes)

The challenges with developing, deploying, and managing AI are better addressed by automating manual data-quality tasks to assure good quality data for AI.

Leveraging cognitive data-quality methods is one way to achieve a level of automation in data validation processes. Cognitive data quality autogenerate the data quality and cleansing routines, thus reducing the need for manual effort. This code can be executed as part of robust and repeatable data preparation control plans. The methods can scan the data, either structured or unstructured, and suggest possible data-quality transformations.

OTHER DATA CONSIDERATIONS FOR AI, MACHINE LEARNING, AND DEEP LEARNING

Utilizing "Alternative Data"

Alternative data is said to be any data gathered from nontraditional data sources—for example, online or geolocation data, sensor data, social media, satellite images, or network data. Increasingly, data used to develop risk models is becoming a blend of traditional and alternative types especially in applications utilizing AI and machine learning.

Typically, traditional data sources are structured and stored in relational databases. In some instances, AI systems employ alternative data that includes unstructured data in the form of real-time transactional data, news feeds, web browsing, geospatial data and so on.

A common data challenge with AI approaches when utilizing larger data volumes is that the time history is not sufficiently long for back-testing purposes (e.g., data capture may have started recently).

The two data types used to build risk models, traditional and alternative, are summarized in Table 2.1. Before we progress to the next parts of this chapter, we wanted to take time to expand on the common steps for "alternative data" before it becomes useful for analytically driven insights and models. Commonly, unstructured "alternative data" must be structured into a more useful tabulated form, so that can it can be combined with existing data used for risk management

Table 2.1 Data Types Used to Generate Risk Models

Type of Data	Definition	Traditional	Alternative
Transactional	▪ Structured and detailed information that captures key characteristics of customer transactions (i.e., installment payments and cash transfers) ▪ Stored in massive online transaction processing (OLTP) relational databases	▪ Aggregated, structured, and typically summarized over longer-term horizons by aggregating into averages etc.	▪ Granular, allowing for open banking aggregation
Internal data	▪ Customer, product, and transactional history	▪ Stored in enterprise databases	▪ Call center data ▪ Digital journeys ▪ App usage

(Continued)

Table 2.1 (Continued)

Type of Data	Definition	Traditional	Alternative
External data	▪ Data available from third-party data providers and public information	▪ For example, positive and negative credit data from a small group of bureaus ▪ Macro-economic information from bureau of statistics	▪ Multiple sources of third-party data (e.g., bureau data, open-banking aggregation, payment data from utilities, purchasing data from online platforms, subscription information, browsing history, weather, and location data) ▪ Public information ▪ Social media data (care is needed if using especially concerning customer consent)
Unstructured data	▪ Data not stored in a predefined structured format	▪ Traditionally required human effort to analyze	▪ Text documents (e.g., emails, web pages, claim forms) ▪ Multimedia content ▪ Network information (i.e., ownership structures, suppliers, liquidity, legal dependencies between counterparties)

purposes, like risk modeling. The process also standardizes the data and reduces its dimensionality. For the inclusion of personal data, the firm will need to implement an information management standard to help govern its use. Such a framework is based on customer or consumer consent, ethical considerations, and regulations, as well as the internal guiding principles of the institution. Furthermore, organizations should also comply with the principles of BCBS239 to "alternative data", as done for the more traditional data.

Extending Risk Data to "Alternative Data" for AI and Machine Learning

Data preparation and its management for risk model development starts with the identification of the relevant data sources. In some cases, these sources need to be justified, which means that the reason for using the data must be evidenced as appropriate for the model to be built without causing bias or unfair outcomes (Figure 2.2).

Importantly, when risk modelers select data sources, there are key organizational processes and policies to be considered. Any such considerations will continue to apply whether AI or machine learning replace traditional risk models or when AI or machine learning augment traditional risk models. The considerations depend on the type of model. Regardless of whether it is a traditional or innovative risk model, it is always good to ensure that the data sources selected are appropriate and justified for the model's intended use. In this case, the intended use refers to the model objective, purpose, and the setting in which the model will be applied. For example, in risk departments, a range of model types are commonly used. A selected set of risk model types are listed and explained below, as well as examples of how risk modelers are utilizing alternative data sources. For example, alternative data from mobile phones and utilities helps lend to the unbanked and underbanked in many countries. This has a significant impact on access to credit for consumers and micro-entrepreneurs, and further helps to ensure fairer access to credit in countries that have historically disadvantaged groups:[1]

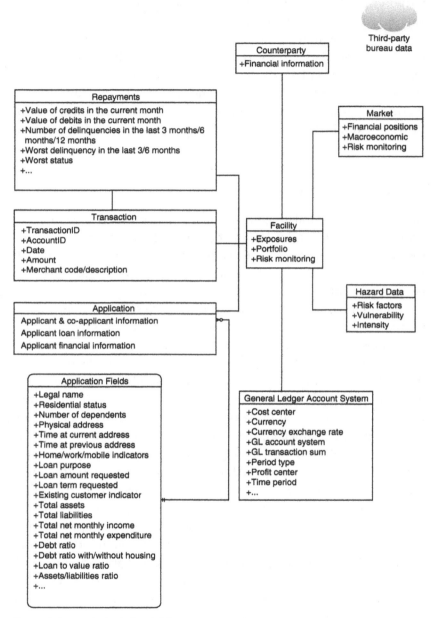

Figure 2.2 A typical relational risk management data model.
The data categories support business as usual (BAU) risk models but are extended for AI/ML models using alternative and third-party data sources.

▪ **Decision models, such as application and behavioral scorecards.** For decision models, risk modelers may use transactional data as a source of alternative data to predict short-term and immediate events like loss of income. By enriching existing data with alternative sources, a more nuanced view of credit risk can be achieved, not only using banking data, but also telecommunications data like subscription data. For more information on the examples, refer to Chapter 3.

▪ **Credit risk parameter estimates for probability of default, loss given default, and exposure at default.** Risk parameters are widely used for regulatory capital, provisions, stress testing, and other internal calculations. Risk modelers are utilizing location data from property intelligence platforms and map applications to develop location scores. Risk modelers then use these scores to improve prediction of probability of default (PD) and loss given default (LGD) models for consumer loan portfolios and loans to small and medium enterprises (SMEs).

▪ **Stress testing.** These are forward-looking analyses to assess how adverse scenarios affect the resilience of a financial institution's balance sheet. This is normally done by stressing macroeconomic variables like GDP (gross domestic product), unemployment rates, and house price indices. A financial institution may take its individual portfolios and granular risk factors and stress its risk parameters using internally defined scenarios. Analysis can be applied to extract insights from news articles and social media to assess sentiment on emerging risks such as geopolitical uncertainty. For climate risk assessments, scenario-based analytics utilize climate scenarios such as those provided by the Network for Greening the Financial System (NGFS).

Synthetic Data Generation

With the use of AI and machine learning and the availability of additional compute power, the use of synthetic data is rising. Often, the available data used for training AI and machine learning has data limitations, such as gaps in the time series, insufficient data history, or in the level of granularity. Simulated data can help overcome these gaps. The methods that are typically applied range from bias adjustments (e.g., the fuzzy method for reject inferencing), repeat sampling (boot-strapping), and synthetic minority oversampling (SMOTE) to those that generate market states like restricted Boltzmann machines.[2]

Some AI and machine learning methods intrinsically generate their own data (generalized adversarial networks, variational auto-encoders). These methods can help stress test models and therefore improve the robustness of models as part of model validation. While these apply to high-dimensional data, it bears noting that by simulating data based on either an algorithmic approach or approximation, additional model risk can be introduced.

Typical Data Preprocessing, Including Feature Engineering

As described previously, AI and machine learning are increasingly leveraged in risk management to augment traditional risk models, because it realizes the long-needed risk transformation to automate mundane tasks and to process large volumes of data.

Getting the data correct for AI and machine learning typically involves standard tasks. Several of these have been covered, such as data quality, cognitive data quality, and extending risk data to "alter-native data". The risk model lifecycle also routinely involves feature engineering and dimensionality reduction.

Feature engineering helps to automatically build a range of features from input data. By using simpler features, AI and machine learning become easier to interpret and, possibly, to maintain over time. Well-engineered features also reduce the effort needed to optimize parame-ters for machine learning. Feature engineering is also important because high-dimensional data often observe sparsity in the data points as the number of inputs grow. This means that as more features are added, the feature space increases.

Certain machine learning algorithms are more sensitive to outliers, meaning that the output model is skewed toward the outlier population. Outliers are not easy to identify in a dataset and take time to interpret. Even well-trained analytics experts require time to explore the data for outliers and to then determine what to do with them. Are they real or due to a bona fide error? Outlier populations can be present in the data used for development of AI and machine learning due to system errors in data, for example, when updates occur, or files of data are transferred between different systems, or due to data entry errors caused by misinterpretation of internal policy, operational processes, and procedures.

It is also important to explore the relationships that exist between outlier populations, as these linked relationships can be helpful to interpret the outliers within, and between, datasets.

There are robust analytical techniques that are helpful to identify outliers. One way includes the use of Principal Components Analysis (PCA). Another unsupervised technique is the use of T-SNE data visualizations. The clusters or "outliers" can be further studied to determine if they are real sub-populations that could be separately modeled, or are outliers due to errors in the dataset.

CONCLUDING REMARKS

For effective data management, organizations rely on effective dataset design and their prevailing risk and control self-assessment frameworks. These include tracking the accuracy, integrity, and completeness of data used for risk measurement and management. Characteristically, although not always, AI approaches tend to utilize higher quantities of data, and therefore data quality and data processing become more prominent. Technology enablers in the form of catalogs, lineage tracking, as well as transparent data and model pipelines enhance the controls and the auditability of data processes.

To fully take advantage of AI and machine learning, current impediments to effective data management can be more easily addressed using automated and repeatable processes.

ENDNOTES

1. Naeem Siddiqi, *When Lending Inequities Fuel Housing Disparities* (Chicago: BAI, 2021).
2. Samuel Cohen, Derek Snow, and Lukasz Szpruch, *Black-Box Model Risk in Finance* (Mathematical Institute, University of Oxford, and The Alan Turing Institute, School of Mathematics, University of Edinburgh, February 9, 2021).

CHAPTER 3

Artificial Intelligence, Machine Learning, and Deep Learning Models for Risk Management

Despite the hype of the last few years, artificial intelligence (AI) and machine learning have proven themselves as useful tools in risk management. As stated earlier, the main reasons are the availability of vast amounts of digital data, greater computing power, and easier access to complex analytics via available modeling tools. More recently, both adoption of digital channels and increase in generated data have accelerated due to the COVID-19 pandemic. This came at a time when financial institutions were already facing myriad internal and external demands:

- Regulatory demands—compliance to new waves of prudential and financial reporting standards
- Macroeconomic demands—sustained low interest rates and inefficiencies putting pressure on profitability and increasing costs, due in part to the inflated cost of compliance
- Technological advancements—advanced analytics, big data, open banking, cloud-based and high-performance computing
- Emerging risks—cyberattacks, those created by the COVID-19 pandemic, climate change, and geopolitical uncertainty
- Digital transformation—challenges to the traditional banking model from new customer demands and the rise of newer, more nimble financial technology companies

Although not without challenges of their own, the use of AI and machine learning is one effective way that organizations can improve their agility to respond to these demands. Some of the benefits of AI and machine learning in risk management include a better, more real-time ability to respond to changes in market conditions and efficiency benefits from automation, while making sense of the copious quantities of data from digitalization.

In speaking to financial institutions and other industry practitioners, the following practical and tangible benefits of AI and machine learning to the risk function were cited:

- **Improved accuracy in predictive modeling and forecasting.** Some studies have also found that AI and machine learning achieve superior accuracy beyond what traditional models achieve (given their ability to rapidly detect nonlinear relationships).

- **Improved handling of big and diverse datasets.** AI and machine learning can handle a diverse range of high-dimensional data, including unstructured data.

- **Challenger models.** AI and machine learning are effective at challenging the status quo by identifying accuracy improvements. In the case of AI and machine learning, a range of algorithms can be utilized.

- **Automate complex risk processes (CCAR (Comprehensive Capital Analysis and Review), CECL/IFRS 9).** AI and machine learning can automate complex risk processes with robotic process automation.

- **Approximate complex risk calculations.** AI and machine learning are effective at approximating complex risk calculations, for example, in derivatives pricing.

- **Improve risk data quality.** AI and machine learning can detect and remediate data quality issues.

- **Risk-based optimization.** AI and machine learning can effectively be applied to optimize based within a set of constraints.

- **Automate steps in the model development process.** AI and machine learning can accelerate the model development process with automated feature engineering and automated machine learning.

Often, when existing models meet current expectations, reluctance in using AI and machine learning is based on this question: "Why use machine learning when my current model are effective at risk profiling, with sufficient performance that is likely to continue for the foreseeable future?" This is a common sentiment, especially in highly regulated industries that have established processes for traditional models in place, and a level of comfort around them. And yes, current models may be effectively designed to respond well to the challenges listed above in estimating risk parameters—traditional models are able to capture nonlinear interactions to some degree. However, there are masked risks that newer approaches of AI and machine learning are better suited for, and are more efficient to identify.

For example, financial technology companies employ AI and machine learning to provide personalized customer experiences and process legal documents. Extreme credit and fraud risk events and other anomalies that represent a small percentage of portfolios are more effectively modeled by machine learning algorithms. Machine learning is also effective at approximating complex risk calculations: a neural network, for example, is sophisticated in its architecture but surprisingly easy to execute. Machine learning is also effective at automating model development tasks such as feature engineering. In the COVID-19 pandemic, organizations have turned to machine learning to adapt to changes in market dynamics—for example, detect early signals of stress by identifying customers with higher repayment difficulty, from more granular transactional data. Furthermore, machine learning can also effectively be applied to segment portfolios into micro-segments.

Innovative models need an innovative approach to risk model development and deployment. With more automation and an accelerated risk model lifecycle, especially in the context of current or impending exogenous events, like COVID-19, risk managers can more quickly respond to dynamic market conditions.

Previously, acceleration was often impeded by additional regulatory demands. Such measures included buffers to expected credit loss provisions due to the uncertainty created by divergent economic data across markets. However, the slowness to develop new models can also be attributed to the manual nature of model development and legacy processes. In addition, technologies that lack repeatable and standardized frameworks can cause bottlenecks in the risk model development cycle. The COVID-19 pandemic provided a means to focus on identifying bottlenecks in model development and decision-making cycles, and this highlighted the need to combine increased automation with a level of human-based decision-making so that organizations can better respond in a forward-looking manner.

The acceleration of risk model development and deployment will enable organizations to develop and deploy more models into production with the same number of staff and timelines compared to models currently in production. More models will also require more automated monitoring processes. They might also need to be reviewed more frequently—potentially daily—to quickly identify any recalibration needs.

This chapter further defines AI and machine learning and includes case studies on how AI and machine learning are used to strengthen risk management. Although the chapter will provide some historical applications of artificial intelligence, machine and deep learning, it also includes practical use cases to demonstrate how machine learning can be leveraged at present.

RISK MODELING USING MACHINE LEARNING

Most of us first started to take notice of AI in 1996 when Deep Blue beat Garry Kasparov in a chess match, and then in 2001 when the IBM Watson Supercomputer famously beat contestants of the game show *Jeopardy*.[1] One of the game show contestants famously joked, "I, for one, welcome our new computer overlords."[2]

With all jokes aside, advanced AI and machine learning are extensively utilized for predictive analytics in cloud-based deployments, and many companies have now embraced its use.[3] Such companies include:

- The global office supply retailer Staples, which created a smart ordering system
- General Motors, which analyzes drivers' preferences and decision-making
- The global pharmaceutical company GlaxoSmithKline (GSK), which enabled customers to ask questions by voice and text via online advertisements
- The University of Southampton, in the United Kingdom, which created a cognitive computing module that offers research modules online

There is also a growing list of Global Systemically Important Banks, Domestic Important Banks, commercial banks, and insurance and financial technology companies that are piloting or have leveraged advanced AI and machine learning to improve customer experience and offer new products and services. The range of applications is wide: from chatbots in call centers to machine learning models used for loan originations and fraud detection to simulating scenarios and synthetic data for stress testing. Today, for many organizations, the use of AI and machine learning is either directly or indirectly involved in risk management processes, risk decision-making, and/or complex risk calculations.

What follows are AI and machine learning stories to highlight the practical ways that financial institutions are using these advanced techniques. However, as there is a tradeoff between complexity and accuracy, the focus for risk management should be on the applications of AI and machine learning where it makes sense. Not every problem is an AI problem. For example, if it makes sense to retain traditional models for regulatory calculations, then there is no need to replace these models with AI and machine learning. In addition, for simple binary target prediction problems where there is little data available, simpler techniques can provide easy solutions.

Tier 1 Commercial Bank in Latin America

A Tier 1 commercial bank, headquartered in Latin America, comprising both retail and wholesale banking operations, had a problem with maintaining asset quality in their loan portfolio, while meeting ambitious growth targets by acquiring new customers. It became especially challenging against a backdrop of rising interest rates and increases in loan-level defaults.

To effectively scale, the bank decided to invest in a new risk modeling platform that operationalized the risk model lifecycle. The platform needed to be robust enough to automate the development and deployment of machine learning models. It became a "machine learning model factory" where highly structured and industrialized model development and deployment processes were put in place. These included data preparation and model development processes, where nonregulatory machine learning models for selected market segments could be developed and automatically deployed into production.

The bank used the opportunity to modernize its technology to also improve its processes. It analyzed each step in its model-building process and identified bottlenecks and their causes. This allowed the bank to improve, for example, model dataset creation from months to days. This delivered an important lesson—simply buying new technology without addressing existing infrastructure, human, or process issues does not yield great results.

The Machine Learning Factory dramatically reduced model development and deployment time from more than 12 months to less than one day. Target markets were able to be segmented at a more granular level, producing better models with more accurate prediction outcomes. A faster, more efficient model lifecycle allowed for more models to be developed and deployed, increasing the number of models under management fivefold. It was achieved by improved model pipeline designs that enabled some machine learning algorithms to update dynamically, with continuous development of challenger models that were used to contest the production champion models. When the challenger was deemed to be better performing, it was deployed into production automatically.

This resulted in better quality of loans and millions of dollars in credit losses avoided. New loans could also be issued with more ease, which enabled expansion of the bank's portfolio across many markets.

Tier 1 Financial Institution in Asia Pacific

Many financial institutions in Asia Pacific are actively using machine learning in nonregulatory settings. One interesting application is the detection of complex transactions that indicate instances of fraud. In some cases, banks are relying on financial technology companies that specialize in AI to build these models. But with easier access to platforms and no-code/low-code interfaces for AI and machine learning, increasingly organizations are developing these themselves.

The occurrence of credit application fraud represents a very small fraction of the population, less than 1%. However, the losses are typically severe. A major concern at a Tier 1 commercial bank in Asia Pacific was that although the number of fraud cases was small, the vast majority bypassed the bank's existing fraud rules. This was a complex problem. The best efforts of the bank, including manual interventions and contacting applicants, meant that some incidents still slipped through the credit- and fraud-checking processes.

To detect the fraudulent behavior, the bank built predictive models based on actual historical data of the approved applications using a gradient boosting machine (GBM). This technique used thousands of decision trees and hundreds of variables as a basis of generating weak prediction models that get ensembled to a final prediction via a score.

Although the GBM models were great at detecting suspicious behavior, the obstacle the bank faced was that the current infrastructure was not robust enough to support the deployment and implementation of advanced machine learning models like GBMs. In the end, the sophistication of the GBM needed to be completely stripped back to a linear model, which meant that the predictive capability was reduced. This story illustrates the potential power of machine learning in improving predictions—but it also reminds us that infrastructure capability needs to be addressed before deploying resources, in the form of funds and time, toward a machine learning project.

Process Automation for Claims Processing

Several organizations have started to use AI and machine learning to develop AI-based behavioral models that can be used to support other applications to improve customer experience. One such model was developed using over a decade of insurance data to find hidden pathways that exist between the question sets asked and the most profitable 20–40 customer segments. Based on the insights of the model, over 30 questions previously used to ascertain medical history were reduced to 7 key questions needed to confirm or deny coverage. What this predictive underwriting capability of the model supplies is faster, easier, and more accurate insurance outcomes that greatly improve the customer experience.

Other AI and machine learning models have been developed to identify the key reason for excluding customers for medical insurance, such as those with a particular type of disability, and whether the excluded population has a higher propensity to make claims at a later point in time. Again, this has contributed to a more efficient underwriting process by reducing time, cost, and paperwork needed to make insurance decisions.

The one condition for all models developed for this project was that it needed to be transparent, meaning that all the inputs and output decisions can be easily explained. The avoidance of "black box" models in favor of those that can be explained easily is a common requirement in financial institutions. As such, explainable AI is a key consideration with any development project and is discussed in greater detail in Chapter 4.

Navigating through the Storm of COVID-19

Like many financial institutions across the globe, a Tier 1 commercial bank in the Asia Pacific region provided repayment holidays to eligible small business customers during the COVID pandemic. Since the customers' risk of default could not be measured using current systems and processes, payments appeared up-to-date due to the referred repayment period, putting the bank at risk. If income were lost during the repayment holiday period, the current behavioral models would not accurately reflect these events, as these models were not designed to predict short-term and immediate events, like a sudden loss of income due to widespread business shutdowns. What this meant is that the current definition of "delinquency" were not a reliable differentiator of risk for small business customers who received deferral arrangements under emergency procedures enacted during COVID-19.

Suddenly, the bank needed to assess how this would affect customer payments, and to do this they turned to machine learning. The bank used data immediately before the COVID-19 pandemic, using 3 months of historical data rather than the 12 months performance window used by the legacy behavioral models. The smaller historical period of 3-months meant that shorter-term variables that are highly impacted by COVID19 needed to be derived, rather than using the long-term drivers of the current models. For the short-term variables, the modelers derived these using advanced feature engineering techniques from customer transactions data, to ensure that recent changes in cash flows could be detected and modeled by the algorithm. Importantly, the transaction data–based feature engineering used income and expense variables highly affected by COVID19. Other variables used in the model included point-in-time ratios, early delinquency at customer group level, and drivers related to velocity of change such as utilization, disposable income, and business-specific risk drivers and self-employment flags. The bank observed that a GBM with a small depth and <100 trees were able to better predict which customers were likely to suffer sudden loss of income events and likely to experience default post-expiry of the COVID-19 holiday repayment scheme.

Approximation of Complex Risk Calculations

Like other sophisticated risk calculations, expected credit loss calculations are typically run as a batch, back-end process. Forward-looking, marginal losses are calculated for a range of scenarios, discounted back to the net present value, and weighted according to the probability of the scenario. If the probability of default has significantly increased since origination, the loan is recognized as stage 2 and lifetime losses are recognized. If not, a 12-month loss is recognized as provision for expected credit loss.

Before deciding on a new loan, what is the expected credit loss under this scenario? This can be approximated using machine learning. The benefit of machine learning is that it can quickly inform the estimated expected credit loss in real time, at the time of loan origination, leading to better decisions.

DEFINITIONS OF AI, MACHINE, AND DEEP LEARNING

Although we have discussed practical use cases of AI and machine learning in risk management, it is also important to appreciate how AI and machine learning is defined, and the major types that are used.

Artificial Intelligence

In 1950, the famous English mathematician Alan Turing asked the question, "Can a machine think?"[4] That question has provoked the computer science domain from its very beginning. Turing's work during World War II on a machine that was able to decipher code from the Nazis' "Enigma" machine provided the edge that the Allied Forces needed to win the war in Europe. The machine underwent several improvements and influenced the development of the first digital computers.

Later in 1955, the American father of AI, the computer scientist John McCarthy, first coined the term *artificial intelligence* while preparing for a conference that explored ways to make machines reason like humans, capable of abstracting thought and solving problems.[5] And this is what AI is essentially about, a computer system that can do tasks that humans need intelligence to do.

In general, AI is often used to describe computer-based systems that can think, learn, and respond to stimuli in their environment. Importantly, like human intelligence, the AI computing system can also subsequently act in response to these stimuli and create its own objective.[6]

Let us further solidify the understanding of AI by taking a purely hypothetical situation of a "paper clip maximizer"[7]: a machine that is programmed to make as many paper clips as possible. What if the machine became intelligent and, like a human, decided to create new paper clips by manufacturing machines to achieve its programmed goal and never stopped production? In this situation, humans may then intervene to create a governance framework to oversee the manufacturing process to ensure that only a million paper clips are created. However, what if, in turn, the paper clip machines decided to check their own work to ensure that they had correctly counted a million paper clips? To achieve this, the machines become self-teaching to make themselves smarter. The now smart and intelligent machines then create new raw-computing material to further check all aspects of the paper clip production that includes constraints (only 1 million paper clips are produced daily). But with each new check, the machines start to question what raw materials work best and so in response, the machines decide to create new raw materials. The result is that the now super-intelligent machines are mimicking every aspect of learning. They display features of intelligence and are thus essentially simulating what it is to be human.[8]

AI has already become deeply embedded in society and used by most of us daily, even if we are not aware. The wide availability of AI is a further tribute to the legacy of McCarthy. McCarthy did not leave us with a collection of theories and exploratory questions on machines and intelligence, but "list processing" (LISP), which was the language of choice for natural language processing (NLP) functions.[9] To this day, LISP remains the standard AI language due to its ability to integrate LISP macros, which are a sequence of instructions that allow control over when and whether arguments are evaluated. More generally, NLP is used by programmers when an AI-enabled system interprets human language in the form of speech and text.[10]

Some great contemporary examples of LISP-enabled AI systems include the voice recognition technology used in iPhone's Siri or Amazon's Alexa that allow mobile devices to interpret essential elements of human language to return an answer.[11] LISP is also used in navigation systems and applications that instantly translate language. Interestingly, from 2016, speech recognition has had profound improvements and has an ever-decreasing error rate. It is also about three times faster than typing text on a mobile phone.[12] Currently, although LISP is used for keyword recognition and text to speech, it tends to be weaker on contextual analysis and informal expressions like "slang" that are used quite commonly in many spoken human languages.

Machine Learning

Machine learning was created by Arthur Samuel at IBM very early in the quest to develop AI. Samuel created a program that had the ability to learn parameters of a function for evaluating the position of checkers on a board during a game of play.[13] Other programmers then created additional methods to enable self-learning by a computer, the most prominent of which is *symbolic AI*.[14] Symbolic AI uses high-level symbolic representations of a problem that are human readable. The symbols are manipulated in an attempt to replicate human intelligence.[15] One of the most successful methods of symbolic AI is so-called production rules that connect symbols to a relationship that shares close similarity to an IF–THEN statement in many programming languages. The system then processes the rules to determine if additional information is needed to solve a problem.[16] However, the symbols can only be used when the input problem is definite.[17] If any uncertainty to the problem exists, as is the case when making a prediction, then a neural network needs to be developed based on "fuzzy logic," which is a type of stochastic search.

Coming back to the definition of machine learning, it is a subset of AI, and over many decades, has matured into a discipline to focus on solvable, practical problems using models and methods borrowed from statistics and probability theory.[18]

In essence machine learning refers to the ability of a machine to learn from data and to keep improving its performance without need of human interference.[19] This means that in the process of a machine learning, a human does not need to continually dictate how to accomplish tasks, while the machine has the ability to utilize an automated self-learning/feedback loop. Machine learning is divided into three broadly defined categories of algorithms: (1) supervised learning, (2) unsupervised learning, and (3) reinforcement learning. Let us further look at each of these.

Supervised Learning

Supervised learning is where machine learning uses learning methods with a target variable to make a prediction.[20] The data used for supervised learning is called *labeled datasets* since it includes the target variable.[21] The labeled data is the training dataset from which the algorithms learn to make new predictions. Large datasets are needed to train supervised learning algorithms.[22] Algorithms that can be used for supervised learning include:[23]

- Gradient boosting machine (GBM)
- Random forest and decision trees
- Naive Bayes classification
- Support vector machines
- Ensemble methods

As an example of how supervised machine learning is used in risk management, machine learning algorithms such as GBM and random forests have been used in decision science applications to improve accuracy and perform well with larger and higher dimensional datasets.

Gradient Boosting Machines

Gradient boosting is an ensemble method for regression and classification problems. It follows a boosted approach, whereby a group of models (weak learners) are combined to form a composite model (strong learner). Gradient boosting uses regression trees for prediction purposes and builds the model iteratively by fitting a model on the residuals. It generalizes by allowing optimization of an objective function.

Random Forests

Random forests are a combination of tree predictors such that each tree depends on a sample (or subset) of the model development data (or training data) selected at random.[24] Working with multiple different sub-datasets can help reduce the risk of overfitting. Random forests or random decision forests are ensemble methods for regression and classification problems based on constructing multiple decision trees and outputting the class that may be either the mode of the classes (classification) or the mean prediction (regression) of the individual trees.

Unsupervised Learning

Unsupervised learning is another category of machine learning, but unlike supervised learning, it uses unlabeled datasets for knowledge discovery. As such, an unsupervised learning algorithm does not include a target variable. The following methods use algorithms to construct understanding of data that allows for machine learning to self-identify patterns in the data:

- Clustering
- Singular value decomposition
- Independent component analysis

Reinforcement Learning

Reinforcement learning differs from both supervised and unsupervised learning as it mimics the way that "agents"—an entity that understands how to make a decision based on past positive and negative experiences—learn by goal-seeking behavior in response to a reward stimulus.[25] It entered the spotlight in 2016 when Google's AI program called AlphaGo beat the 18-time world champion of the game Go.[26] A notable example that is often used to describe reinforcement learning is a *grid world*, where a robot is in a particular cell, say cell 2,3, and receives an instruction to let it know what cell it is in. In this context, the robot is capable of four possible subsequent actions: either to move one cell up, right, down, or left. The robot is assigned a negative point (–1) whenever it hits a wall of the grid or moves into a blocked cell, but it receives a positive award when it moves into a cell marked as goal. If the robot is moved to a random cell and then moves in a manner to increase its chances to receive a positive reward, then it has displayed features of learning. An example of reinforcement learning in risk management is in collections path treatment development. Here, the goals is set to maximize dollars recovered while minimizing costs of collections.

Reinforcement learning works well when humans can specify the goal but are uncertain about the optimal path.[27]

Deep Learning

The machine learning approaches described thus far have limitations in that they rely on a programmer to determine what is informative for making a decision that can achieve a preset goal.[28] This means that the machine learning algorithm is dependent on the programmer and thus programmer insight. Furthermore, the machine learning approaches and algorithms previously described have all demonstrated to reach a definable plateau in their performance as the amount of data increases.

This is not the case with a more scalable machine learning algorithm referred to as *deep learning* where performance relies on large amounts of data to build models more accurately.[29] Essentially, deep learning is performed when nets of neural networks that resemble layers are utilized for learning. Classes of deep learning include: (1) convolutional neural networks that analysts widely use for image recognition and classification, and (2) recurrent neural networks for sequence data like time series, text, speech, etc. The other side is that deep learning is not suited to smaller datasets used to develop traditional machine learning models.[30]

The reason deep learning does not deteriorate in terms of performance as the size of data increases is because the algorithms are able to learn independently by identifying structures in data (Figure 3.1). It then focuses on parts of these structures to achieve a goal.[31] The power of deep learning is derived by use of a computing model that is inspired by the human brain[32] and imitates the most basic biological processes of a brain cell, called the neuron, that in the brain contributes to learning and memory. Let us take a second to explain the neuron to better appreciate the biology that underpins the artificial process of deep learning. The human brain contains 8.6 billion fundamental units of nerve cells called neurons[33] and these cells are highly specialized to transmit information.[34] The 8.6 billion neurons are crammed into about 1.2L volume of brain tissue and form a vast network in that small space.[35] Neurons are composed of a main body with very tiny extensions that branch off the main body called dendrites. An impulse transmits along dendrites to the information center of the cell body or to a dendrite of a neighboring neuron.[36]

To mimic the complexity of the biological neuronal network of the brain and create a deep learning model, the artificial neuron works like a biological cell where it receives a set of inputs (x) or impulses, each of which is assigned a specific weight (w). The neuron then computes numerous functions (y) on each of the now weighted inputs.[37] Weights assigned are not arbitrary and derived by training a neuron, achieved by showing neurons a large number of training examples. These are iteratively changed to reduce error on the training examples.

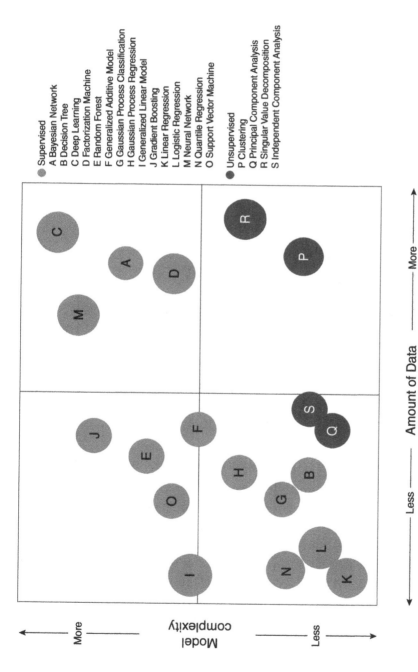

Figure 3.1 Deep learning is the most complex form of supervised machine learning. It can scale because there are no performance limitations as the amount of data used for training increases. Also shown in the graph are other supervised and unsupervised machine learning algorithms/techniques. The size of the bubbles indicates complexity relative to others within each quadrant.

Supervised
A Bayesian Network
B Decision Tree
C Deep Learning
D Factorization Machine
E Random Forest
F Generalized Additive Model
G Gaussian Process Classification
H Gaussian Process Regression
I Generalized Linear Model
J Gradient Boosting
K Linear Regression
L Logistic Regression
M Neural Network
N Quantile Regression
O Support Vector Machine

Unsupervised
P Clustering
Q Principal Component Analysis
R Singular Value Decomposition
S Independent Component Analysis

Amount of Data

Less — More

Model complexity

More

Less

A classical challenge is overfitting. It is possible that a neural network becomes overfitted where the model produced by the algorithm perfectly performs each time on the training sample but fails in practice. The issue of overfitting occurs when too many parameters have been used and not enough training data points.[38] The problem can be overcome by either adding more training samples that can run into the hundreds of thousands, sometimes millions, of data points,[39] or by reducing the connectedness between neurons.[40]

The way in which the weighted inputs are computed depends on the type of activation function used. An activation function is a mathematical transformation that acts as the transfer function: it translates the input signal to the output signal. The more common activation functions used are:

- Identity functions that are linear. The value of the argument used for training is not changed and its range is potentially not bounded.
- Sigmoidal functions are S-shaped like logistic and hyperbolic tangent (or tanh) functions that produce bounded values with a range of 0 to 1, or −1 to 1.
- Softmax functions are multiple logistic functions and are a generalized representation of logistic regression that forces the sum of their values to be 1.
- Value functions are bell-shaped functions such as a Gaussian function.
- Exponential and reciprocal functions are bounded by 0 and 1.

Linear activation functions take a linear combination of each weighted input, while nonlinear activation functions like the sigmoidal function take a sum of the weighted inputs into a logistic function. For example, when learning the sigmoidal logistic function initially approximates an exponential equation. Please note that these intrinsic characteristics of the sigmoidal logistic function are not to be confused with machine learning optimization discussed in Chapter 8. Furthermore, with a sigmoidal neuron, the value that gets returned is between 0 and 1 and is dependent on the weighed input that gets summed.

For instance, if the weighed sum is negative, then the returned value is close to "0." Despite their limitation, sigmoidal neurons are used more often than linear neurons, as the generated algorithms are much more versatile in comparison.[41]

Neurons are also the building blocks of the entire nervous system of the body and receive sensory information from the external environment and send commands to muscles among many other known functions.[42] The functionality of the neuron is extremely complex, and the complexity in turn stimulates active areas of research and development that could, at some point, further augment and drive new ways of approaching and applying deep learning along the road to replicate human intelligence.

Artificial Neural Networks

An artificial neural network in a deep learning algorithm is created in an analogous manner to a biological neural network in that its creation is dependent on many interactions: from the input data, between many neurons, and the output generated from the neural network's response. Deep learning algorithms are further complicated by nets of neural networks that resemble layers. Neurons at the input layer are connected to the actual output or answer to the problem and need not connect to each other, while neurons at the output layer are connected to one another and directly receive input data. The network can be feed-forward where there are no connections between neurons at the input to those at the output layer, or recursive where there are connections between input and output layers[43] (Figure 3.2).

There can also be a hidden layer that exists between the input and output layers. The hidden layer itself is where the wondrous power of the network solves problems and derive features of the input data that are extracted to learn and derive an output. Technically, the hidden layer involves an extra transformation of some type but requires no extra parameters. Interestingly, the hidden layer is where the "deep" aspect of deep learning gets derived—a neural network with many hidden layers is considered "deep."[44] The most popular form of a neural network is a multilayer perceptron (MLP)

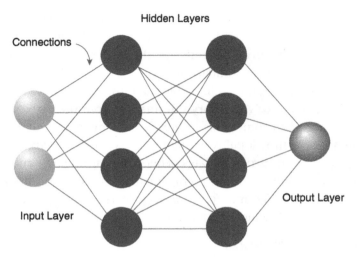

Figure 3.2 Schema of an artificial neural network with hidden layers.

that has any number of inputs, usually at least one hidden layer, and many neurons in each hidden layer. The MLP can have a different number of neurons in each hidden layer and has weights between the following:

- The input layer and first hidden layer
- One hidden layer to the next hidden layer when there is more than one hidden layer
- The last hidden layer and the output

Automated Machine Learning

There are now platforms available that offer automated machine learning (AutoML). These offer predeveloped model templates for a range of algorithms. This allows the predefined model pipelines to run in parallel against a training dataset and automate, train, and evaluate predictive accuracy of each model, with very little human intervention required. AutoML is useful when modelers are not certain of choice of algorithm.

Overall, AutoML allows for fewer assumptions to be made by a modeler by evaluating different model pipelines to find the most predictive model for the dataset, so that the best predictive models that are the best fit for the dataset are developed. Model pipelines can be based on templates that can include data processing, apply regulatory constraints and check for bias and fairness of model outcomes. In addition, the models generated by AutoML still need review and justification, including explaining both the interpretations and decisions are fair, safe, and transparent. We explain these considerations in Chapters 4 and 5.

A Further Note: Robotic Process Automation

Once a machine has been taught to solve a problem, the resulting logic can then be deployed—this is the aim of a machine learning algorithm. When deployment of the machine replaces a business process, is truly self-sustaining, and requires little human intervention, then that automation is referred to as robotic process automation (RPA). In some cases, RPA is successfully deployed to replace the traditional strategies of cost savings, such as offshoring and outsourcing business operations.[45]

RPA has started to replace traditional cost-saving strategies because it is estimated in some cases to run at a much lower total cost of a typical human resources. In addition, RPA has been shown to dramatically reduce processing time and eliminate error rates.[46] Interestingly, the International Foundation of Robotics published that the use of robotics has nearly doubled over five years, and as of December 2021 there are now 126 robots per 10,000 employees. There are many examples of RPA in the insurance industry where the process of claim forms that once took workers four days to complete has been cut to a mere two hours.[47]

Putting It All Together

To summarize the terms of reference[48] AI is referred to as the "superset" and was the first to be discovered in the 1950s. It has rapidly evolved and expanded ever since. Machine learning is a subset of AI and was created as part of our continuing quest to simulate human intelligence. Although deep learning was discovered soon after machine learning, its power and scalability had to wait for appropriate computing power.[49] Deep learning is an innermost subset, being a class of machine learning that utilizes layers of neural networks that enable complex tasks like computer vision.

CONCLUDING REMARKS

AI and machine learning are progressing rapidly in the financial services industry around the globe. However, it should be noted that some countries have much slower rates of adoption due to the unease around its use for regulatory compliance purposes.[50] Companies in some countries are embracing AI and machine learning at rates that are half of that compared with global peers. As such, it has been argued that these countries need to double their pace of AI and machine learning to reap the benefits, estimated at $15.7 trillion to be added to the global economy by 2030.[51] However, financial institutions must have an action plan for extending their use of innovative, advanced techniques, while ensuring that the fundamentals to manage the risk model lifecycle, including data management, and quality and robust infrastructure to support deployment are in place.

ENDNOTES

1. Jo Best, "IBM Watson: The inside story of how the *Jeopardy*-winning supercomputer was born, and what it wants to do next," *TechRepublic*, (CBS Interactive, 2013); C. Mercer, "Which companies are using Watson's big data and analytics to power their business?" *Computerworld* (2018).

2. John Markoff, "Computer Wins on *Jeopardy!*: Trivial, It's Not," *New York Times* (February 16, 2011).

3. Mercer, Which companies are using Watson's big data and analytics to power their business?

4. Alan Turing, "Computing machinery and intelligence," *Mind: A quarterly review of psychology and philosophy* IX(236) (1950); Rebecca Jacobson, "8 things you didn't know about Alan Turing," *PBS News Hour* (2014).

5. Martin Childs, *John McCarthy: Computer scientist known as the father of AI* (Kensington, London: Independent, 2011).

6. Anand S. Rao, Gerard Verweij, and E. Cameron, *Sizing the Prize—What's the Real Value of AI for Your Business and How Can You Capitalise?* (Boston: Pricewaterhouse-Coopers, 2017).

7. Nick Bostrom, *Superintelligence: Paths, Dangers, Strategies* (Oxford United Kingdom: Oxford University Press, 2016).

8. Childs, *John McCarthy*.

9. Sarah Butcher, *The Ancient Programming Language That Will Get You an AI Job in Finance* (New York: efinancial careers, 2017).

10. Childs, *John McCarthy*; Margot O'Neill, Explainer: What is artificial intelligence? (Sydney, NSW, Australia: ABC News, 2017).

11. Sarah Butcher, *The Ancient Programming Language That Will Get You an AI Job in Finance* .

12. Erik Brynjolfsson and Andrew McAfee, "The business of artificial intelligence—What it can and cannot do for your organization," *Harvard Business Review* (July 18, 2017).

13. Arthur L. Samuel, "Some Studies in Machine Learning Using the Game of Checkers," *IBM Journal of Research and Development* 3:211–229 (July 1959); Nils J. Nilsson et al., *An Introduction to Machine Learning—An Early Draft of a Proposed Textbook*. 1st ed. (Stanford, CA: Robotics Laboratory, Department of Computer Science, Stanford University, 1998).

14. Allen Newell and Herbert Simon, "Computer science as empirical inquiry: Symbols and search," *Communications of the ACM* 19(3)(1976): 113–126; Nilsson, *An Introduction to Machine Learning*.

15. Nilsson, *An Introduction to Machine Learning*.

16. Newell and Simon, *Computer Science as Empirical Inquiry*, 113–126.

17. Newell and Simon, *Computer Science as Empirical Inquiry*, 113–126; Nilsson, *An Introduction to Machine Learning*.

18. Pat Langley, "The changing science of machine learning," *Machine Learning* 82(3) 2011): 275–279.

19. Brynjolfsson and McAfee, The business of artificial intelligence.

20. O. Zhao, *AI, Machine Learning and Deep Learning Explained* (New York: ElectrifAI, 2017).

21. J. Le, *Algorithms, Machine Learning, Supervised Learning, Unsupervised Learning* (Detroit, MI: KD Nuggets, 2016); Zhao, *AI, Machine Learning and Deep Learning Explained*.

22. Le, *Algorithms, Machine Learning, Supervised Learning, Unsupervised Learning*.

23. Le, *Algorithms, Machine Learning, Supervised Learning, Unsupervised Learning*; Zhao, *AI, Machine Learning and Deep Learning Explained*.

24. Leo Breiman, *Random Forests* (Berkeley: Statistics Department, University of California–Berkeley, 2001).

25. Nilsson, *An Introduction to Machine Learning*.

26. Zhao, *AI, Machine Learning and Deep Learning Explained*.

27. Brynjolfsson and McAfee, The business of artificial intelligence.

28. Nikhil Buduma, *Deep Learning in a Nutshell—What It Is, How It Works, Why Care?* (Detroit, MI: KDnuggets, 2015); Brynjolfsson and McAfee, The business of artificial intelligence.

29. Zhao, *AI, Machine Learning and Deep Learning Explained*.

30. Brynjolfsson and McAfee, The business of artificial intelligence.

31. Buduma, *Deep Learning in a Nutshell*; D. Petereit, *AI, Machine Learning and Deep Learning Explained* (Hanover, Germany: CEBIT, Deutsche Messe, 2017).

32. Buduma, *Deep Learning in a Nutshell*; D. Petereit, *AI, Machine Learning and Deep Learning Explained*; Zhao, *AI, Machine Learning and Deep Learning Explained*.

33. Suzana Herculano-Houzel, "The human brain in numbers: A linearly scaled-up primate brain," *Frontiers in Human Neuroscience* 3(31) (2009).

34. Kenneth S. Kosik, "Life at low copy number: How dendrites manage with so few mRNAs," *Neuron* 92(6) (December 21, 2016): 1168–1180.

35. Herculano-Houzel, The human brain in numbers.

36. Kosik, Life at low copy number, 1168–1180.

37. Buduma, *Deep Learning in a Nutshell.*

38. Buduma, *Deep Learning in a Nutshell.*

39. A. Copeland, *Deep Learning Explained—What It Is, and How It Can Deliver Business Value to Your Organisation* (Santa Clara, CA: NVIDIA Deep Learning, 2016).

40. Buduma, *Deep Learning in a Nutshell.*

41. Buduma, *Deep Learning in a Nutshell.*

42. Herculano-Houzel, The human brain in numbers; Kosik, Life at low copy number, 1168–1180.

43. Buduma, *Deep Learning in a Nutshell.*

44. Zhao, *AI, Machine Learning and Deep Learning Explained.*

45. Shane O'Sullivan and Brandon Stafford, *RPA and Your Digitisation Strategy* (Sydney, NSW, AUS: PricewaterhouseCoopers, 2016).

46. O'Sullivan and Stafford, *RPA and Your Digitisation Strategy.*

47. Jared Wade, *RPA in Action: Innovative Ways Five Financial Services Companies Are Using Automation* (Amsterdam, Netherlands: Finance TnT, 2018).

48. Zhao, *AI, Machine Learning and Deep Learning Explained.*

49. Copeland, *Deep Learning Explained*; Zhao, *AI, Machine Learning and Deep Learning Explained.*

50. Lin Evlin and Margot O'Neill, Australia must embrace AI revolution with automation set to affect every job, report says, *Lateline,* (Sydney, AUS: ABC News, August 8, 2017), https://www.abc.net.au/news/2017-08-08/australia-must-embrace-ai-revolution-alphabeta-report/8774044

51. Rao and Verweij, *Sizing the Prize.*

CHAPTER 4

Explaining Artificial Intelligence, Machine Learning, and Deep Learning Models

Due to the black box nature of some, not all, artificial intelligence (AI) and machine learning algorithms, the model logic and the subsequent decisions are often hard to explain. This inability to explain the modeling approach, mechanics, and limitations may apply to both a technical and nontechnical stakeholder. For example, a model validator will want to assess that the model is performing as expected, while senior management will want to understand what will happen if the model produces incorrect predictions. In both cases, if the functional form of the model does not lend itself to human intuition, and/or the model development process is opaque, these questions become difficult to answer.

Firstly, considering the model logic, for some AI and machine learning, the lack of explainability stems from the complex engineered features that may include sophisticated and nonlinear transformations. In this case, the machine-created model inputs and modeled relationships between inputs lack human intuition.

In some cases, the lack of explainability stems from the model optimization process that is driven by the model itself rather than human intelligence, which means that the "learning" of the model is often captured within the model rather than by a human.

In a speech,[1] Governor Lael Brainard of the Federal Reserve highlighted the benefits of AI and machine learning of greater accuracy and speed and the enabling ability of AI to adapt in near real-time. She defined the black-box problem of AI and machine learning as complex models lacking transparency. The lack of transparency is attributed to the model development process that is defined and specified by a machine or data-driven rather than a human, comparing, say, a deep learning neural network to an econometric or other statistical model. We will discuss selected methods that are applied to optimize machine learning algorithms in Chapter 8. It may be challenging to decipher the choices for parameters, as well as the choices for justifiable data sources and inputs.

The complexity of AI and machine learning is both strength and weakness. It makes the models very flexible to detect nonlinear interactions and correlations, but also more prone to model spurious relationships in the training data, otherwise known as overfitting. In some cases, complexity is associated with opacity. Therefore, there is a trade-off between the opacity of the algorithm and its business benefits—for example, improved accuracy or efficiency.

AI and machine learning algorithms are said to utilize fewer statistical assumptions but optimize hyperparameters based on an objective function.[2] This property allows for the model development process to be done with less human intervention.

In general, models, analytical algorithms, and quantitative computations used in risk management are subject to strict regulatory guidance, like the independent assessment of the conceptual soundness of the analytical approach. The lack of inherent explainability of AI and machine learning raises a fundamental question: How can we assess the conceptual soundness of a model that is hard to explain?

In addition, with a model that lacks explainability, it is difficult to foresee any unintended consequences from model usage, and this increases the operational risk when implementing the model in production. With AI and machine learning, process audit and oversight of the model development process become more prominent.

A lack of explainability impedes not only the ability to explain the model logic but also the individual decisions made by the model. This is an important aspect in areas where consumer protection laws are in operation (such as credit decisions where reason codes are required) or other highly regulated industries.

Like a colleague would say, "*. . .it's a bit like Schrodinger's cat—the black box is not transparent, we therefore don't know if the cat is alive or not.*" Of course, there are explainability diagnostics to help with that. An overview of these is provided in a subsequent section.

DIFFERENCE BETWEEN EXPLAINING AND INTERPRETING MODELS

Explaining an AI or machine learning refers to the ability of a human to describe the most important model inputs and draw inferences on why the model predictions are what they are. To explain the model, the inferences need not be exact. In this case, the models can also be explained in general terms: the degree of changes to model inputs and associated magnitude of the expected changes in outputs. On the one hand, there is no guarantee that the answer will exactly match the expectations of users or consumers, or that the results are reproducible. On the other hand, if a model is interpretable, then the mathematical function can be directly interpreted by a human, as well as the method for how the model uses the inputs to derive the outputs. There is a guarantee that the model calculations are transparent, and the output is reproducible.

Based on their context and purpose, for many high-stakes decisions in the risk management domain, algorithms must be both explainable and interpretable.

In many instances, risk models require approval from internal and external stakeholders. For example, highly material risk models used for market risk, liquidity, and capital adequacy require an assessment of their conceptual soundness, approval and sign-off from both an independent model validation function internal to a firm and from the external regulator. At the same time, in some parts of the world, models used for credit decisions require financial services providers to supply reason codes to loan applicants to inform them why they have been denied credit and when using post-hoc explanations to validate their accuracy (see, for example, regulatory requirements pertaining to the Equal Credit Opportunity Act and Regulation B,[3] Consumer Financial Protection Bureau[4]). The challenge it poses with credit decisions relates to underwriting and other processes across the credit risk management cycle, where alignment with the lending policy and fair lending laws are required. These include loan onboarding, account management, collections management, on so on. For example, traditional regression-based models and decision trees are interpretable and self-explanatory. However, more complex models such as neural networks, gradient boosting, and ensemble methods have some ability to be explained (like visualizing the weights of nodes in the neural network) but are not always fully interpretable.

There are also auxiliary areas in risk management where models can be used that do not require approval from at least an internal validation and governance team nor adhere to consumer protection laws. These blind-spot areas can feed into assessments and decisions impacting consumers, and therefore, although these models need not necessarily be interpretable, any model, whether AI and machine learning-based or traditional, needs to be subject to a governance framework.

WHY EXPLAIN AI MODELS

Risk models are typically used for high-priority decisions subject to regulatory requirements. It is therefore important that a range of stakeholders, from risk managers to senior management to external regulators, can have confidence in the use of the models and their outputs. However, with AI and machine learning, it is often difficult to understand the model and its components.

Often, the lack of explainability is further exacerbated by organizational silos and a lack of holistic visibility across the model lifecycle of AI and machine learning. Today, the lack of transparency inhibits a firm's ability to appropriately manage their risk models and associated model risk, which has led to a degree of distrust of AI and machine learning.

Some of the main challenges associated with the ability to explain risk models are:

- An inability to explain the algorithmic functions and quantitative methods and how the model output is produced.
- A lack of transparency in the model development process and assumptions.
- An inability to explain or prove that the data that was used to derive a model and subsequent decision is justifiable.
- A lack of confidence in how the model will behave on data outside of its calibration range.
- A lack of a holistic framework for AI and machine learning governance.
- An inability to assess for the degrees of overfitting, bias, fairness, and other unintended consequences.

■ Lack of access to the model documentation that includes the details of the specification and assumptions leading to an inability to manage and maintain the models, and therefore manage its associated model risk appropriately.

The overwhelming speed of development and dynamic calibration can lead to a resistance by internal and external stakeholders to accept and approve the model. Of course, the level of explainability that is needed will also be decided by the context in which the model will be used and the materiality of the models.

As a starting point, it is important to determine what the model will be used for and who would be responsible and accountable. Then, define who the stakeholders are and what they need to know. Here are some questions that can be asked relevant to a diverse set of stakeholders:

■ Do they need to know what will happen if the model gets it wrong?

■ Do they need to know that the drivers are justifiable and aligned to the business aim?

■ Do they need to know that the model is performing well and stable over time?

■ Do they need to know how the model works?

■ Do they need to know how the model fits into the business process?

■ Do they need to know the process followed for feature engineering?

■ Do they need to know which features are driving the predictions? Or which features mattered in individual predictions?

■ Do they need to know the performance differences between the AI and machine learning model and a simpler benchmark model?

■ Do they need to know that the model is parsimonious, that is, that it is as simple as possible, yet has a high degree of predictive power?

This is a good starting point to explain the characteristics of the model in a well-rounded way to make the AI and machine learning as accessible as possible to a range of stakeholders.

COMMON APPROACHES TO ADDRESS EXPLAINABILITY OF DATA USED FOR MODEL DEVELOPMENT

As mentioned in Chapter 2, the right data governance framework is crucial for successful and responsible AI and machine learning. This section further emphasizes the importance of standardized and consistent data management processes to improve trust, transparency and governance of AI and machine learning.[5]

Data management refers to the process of accessing, acquiring, transforming, and preparing input data for analysis. To aid in the transparency of the model, processes that relate to the data collection, data preparation and quality validation, as well as feature engineering need to be transparent, reproducible (in some cases), robust, and well documented.

The use of justifiable inputs for model development will help foster trust in AI and machine learning systems.

Data-centric questions related to the data collection processes are:

- Are the data sources reliable, meaningful, and justifiable?
- Do I have standardized data quality, validation, and sampling processes in place?
- Is my model using training data that is free from bias and representative of the population that the model will be applied to (i.e., are minority groups over-/underrepresented)?

Data-centric questions related to variable selection processes are:

- What is the methodology followed for variable selection and reduction?
- Do I have the methods/approaches to variable selection and reduction documented?
- What is the mix between automated processes and human judgment?

Data-centric questions related to feature engineering are:

- Will the production systems support the feature engineering logic?

■ Are the methods/approaches to feature engineering automated and supported by my model risk policy?

■ Are the processes reproducible using either a down-the-middle sample or sample of recent production data?

COMMON APPROACHES TO ADDRESS EXPLAINABILITY OF MODELS AND MODEL OUTPUT

Explainable AI is a multidisciplinary scientific field with dedicated resources and methods specific to the respective domain and subject areas. In this section, we will highlight a few approaches and methods that are popular in the risk management domain.

First, we distinguish between intrinsic and model-agnostic explainability.

There are AI and machine learning that exist today that are fully explainable and interpretable. We can say, interpretable risk models are intrinsically explainable (e.g., decision trees and regression methods). In some instances, for risk management, several authors reason that these are preferred for models impacting consumers or models that are regulated.[6]

Of course, in some cases, complex models offer accuracy improvements. Risk modelers may also opt to improve the explainability of complex models by applying constraints to inputs. During the model development process, modelers may add constraints to features to maintain domain-specific rules (e.g., developing neural networks with constrained monotonicity, additivity, linearity, or smoothness).[7]

Another area of focus is model-agnostic explainability. Model-agnostic explainability methods are independent of the modeling algorithm and typically applied after model development. There are different model-agnostic methods used to address the various aspects of a lack of explainability in AI and machine learning. Table 4.1 summarizes how several important model-agnostic methods can be applied, depending on the questions being asked of the model and its inputs.

Several of the methods included in Table 4.1 can be applied as post-hoc explanations to better understand the model logic. Such

Table 4.1 Model-agnostic Methods as Techniques That Can Be Applied to Address Model-Related Questions

Question	Model-agnostic Technique	Type
What are the most important features?	Variable importance Relative variable importance	Global
How do the drivers work?	Partial dependence Individual conditional expectation Saliency maps	Global/Local
What is the explanation for a particular prediction?	Local interpretable model-agnostic explanations Shapley values	Local
What needs to change to get a different outcome for a particular prediction?	Counterfactuals Adversarial testing	Local
How robust is the model to changes in the feature space?	Sensitivity analysis Stress testing	Global

methods can be applied at both the global and local level. A global method applies to the dataset while a local method explains the model outcome for an observation or for a particular prediction.

Post-hoc explanations include global interpretability methods such as feature importance and partial dependence, as well as local interpretability methods such as Shapley values, individual conditional explanations, and local interpretable model-agnostic explanations. These will be explained next.

1. Partial dependence plots

   PDP (partial dependence plots) show the functional relationship between the input and the prediction. It achieves this by perturbing the values of a single feature to depict the average prediction of the model for the range of values of the feature. (See Figure 4.1.)

2. Individual conditional explanations

   Like partial dependence plots, but in this case, individual conditional explanations track the average prediction at the individual or local level. ICE plots are also helpful to detect interactions. (See Figure 4.2.)

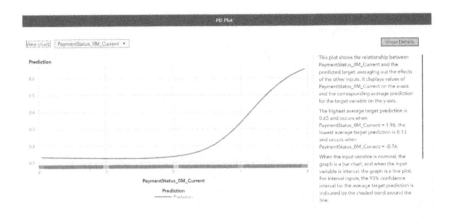

Figure 4.1 Example of a partial dependency plot explaining the functional relationship between the feature and the labeled variable (at the global level).

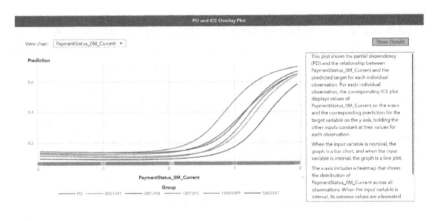

Figure 4.2 Example of an individual conditional explanation at the local level.

3. Shapley values

Shapley values have their roots in game theory and explain the contributions of the features to a prediction by averaging across permutations. A benefit of Shapley values is that it attributes individual feature effects to the overall prediction in an additive way: the Shapley values sum up to the overall prediction for

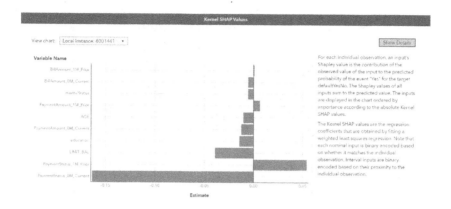

Figure 4.3 Example of Shapley values at the local level.

the instance. As it is additive, it is intuitive and can help explain the drivers behind an individual prediction. (See Figure 4.3.)

4. Saliency maps

Saliency maps, as shown in Figure 4.4, are heat maps that use color to indicate the region in the feature space that is contributing to the prediction. It is a popular method in computer vision.

5. Local interpretable model-agnostic explanations

LIME (local interpretable model-agnostic explanations) explains the predictions of any model by building a local interpretable surrogate model.[8] As a first step, the method samples the feature space in the region of an individual observation. Then, a sparse linear regression model, such as LASSO, is trained on this generated sample, using the predictions that are produced by the pretrained model as a target. Namely, the surrogate model approximates the behavior of the black-box model at the local level, as the regression coefficients can be interpreted directly. (See Figure 4.5.)

6. Counterfactual analysis

A counterfactual explanation of a prediction (assuming a causal relationship) describes the smallest change to the feature values that changes the prediction to a predefined output.[9]

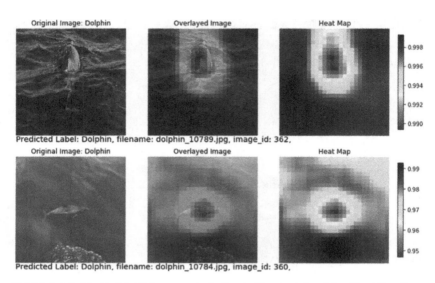

Figure 4.4 Example of a saliency map typically used in computer vision (See https://go.documentation.sas.com/doc/en/pgmsascdc/9.4_3.5/casdlpg/n0rkb1a1p6r6kpn-141f6yxzfaawj.htm).

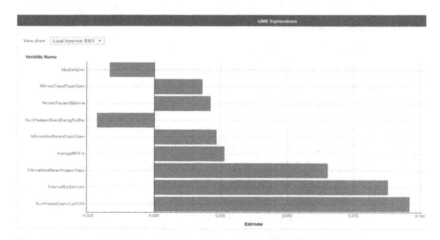

Figure 4.5 Example of a local interpretable model-agnostic explanations (LIME).

In AI and machine learning, counterfactual analysis is used to derive explanations[10] and assess fairness,[11] and the robustness of models.[12]

7. Local rule-based explanations

Like LIME, LORE (local rule-based explanations) explains the predictions of any model by building a local interpretable surrogate model as a set of decision rules that can help explain the reasons for a decision. In addition, it generates a set of counterfactual rules that explain the changes to the features that will lead to a different outcome.[13]

8. Accumulated local effects

ALE (accumulated local effects) plots extend PDP by handling feature correlations.[14] Put simply, instead of averaging the predictions as is done in PDP, ALE accumulates the differences in the predictions.

9. Model stability/sensitivity analysis

Sensitivity or stability analysis is used to stress test the model by assessing the performance and behavior of a model on data ranges not captured by the training data. This can be done by using synthetic data to assess model robustness. A common technique is synthetic minority oversampling technique (SMOTE), or by applying noise perturbation to the weights of neural network to evaluate changes to the neural network with respect to accuracy.

10. Adversarial testing

There are machine learning algorithms that are more vulnerable to an adversarial attack. Adversarial attacks are intentionally designed to cause models to misclassify. This can occur during or after the model development. To further explain how an adversarial attack can occur:

- During model development, machine learning is trained to optimize based on consistent statistical distributions.
- An adversary will introduce data to the model that violates the mentioned statistical assumption to diminish model accuracy or lead to undesirable outcomes.

Several defenses can be applied, such as detection methods including Shapley values that are computed at the internal layers of a deep neural network. These can discriminate between normal and adversarial inputs. Another option is to train a model on data that includes adversarial examples so that the model is more robust to this form of attack.

11. Attribution analysis

The outcomes of two different scenarios of the machine learning are compared (for example, a change in inputs or logic) or data from two different time periods. This allows for an understanding of the drivers behind differences in measures of model performance. In other words, it allows modelers to better understand how changes to model inputs have impacted model performance or predictions made by the model. For example, comparing a development sample with the first three months of pre-production data prior to the model being fully productionized.

LIMITATIONS IN POPULAR METHODS

Several authors and industry bodies highlighted the limitations of post-hoc explainability diagnostics.[15]

A limitation of post-hoc explanations is that it only partially interprets the model and may therefore be misleading. In other instances, it relies on the accuracy of the underlying surrogate model.

One way to think about post-hoc explainability techniques is by looking at your friends' vacation photos. Each picture tells a story of where they have been and the environment they found themselves in. One picture might be in front of the Eiffel Tower and another of a casual stroll down the Champs-Élysées (one of the most recognizable streets in the world), and another is the Mona Lisa. Can you safely and confidently infer, only by looking at the pictures, that your friends did indeed visit Paris?

Similarly, post-hoc diagnostics supply different lenses looking at the same multidimensional object. Each diagnostic supplies a unique perspective. When the different lenses are combined, it is possible to achieve a better understanding of the functioning of the model.

However, keep in mind that by adding another layer of complexity in the form of post-hoc diagnostics to an already complex model, it may further increase model complexity and therefore increase model risk.

CONCLUDING REMARKS

Explainable AI (XAI) is now an established discipline and will continue to evolve. According to Christoph Molnar, explainability is the catalyst for large-scale adoption of AI and machine learning. As the use of AI and machine learning matures, so will the techniques that describe them.[16]

Risk models are often used for critical (and therefore highly regulated) decisions. It is therefore important that a range of stakeholders, from risk managers to senior management to external regulators, can trust the model and its outputs.

Looking ahead, the ability to explain various aspects of a model to a range of stakeholders will extend beyond the use of post-hoc diagnostics, to using natural language interpretation, as well as visualization—to explain the model in nontechnical terms, to models that explain and self-document themselves.

ENDNOTES

1. Governor Lael Brainard, "Supporting Responsible Use Of Ai And Equitable Outcomes In Financial Services," *Board of Governors of the Federal Reserve, AI Academic Symposium, Washington, DC* (virtual event), (January 12, 2021), https://www.federalreserve.gov/newsevents/speech/brainard20210112a.htm

2. Peter Quell, Anthony Graham Bellotti, Joseph L. Breeden, and Javier Calvo Martin, "Machine Learning and Model Risk Management, version 1.0," *Model Risk Managers' International Association* (8 March 2021), https://mrmia.org/wp-content/uploads/2021/03/Machine-Learning-and-Model-Risk-Management.pdf

3. Code of Federal Regulations, *Part 1002, Equal Credit Opportunity Act (Regulation B)*, (last updated June 6, 2022), https://www.ecfr.gov/current/title-12/chapter-X/part-1002

4. *Consumer Financial Protection Bureau Acts to Protect the Public from Black-Box Credit Models Using Complex Algorithms* (26 May 2022), https://www.consumerfinance.gov/about-us/newsroom/cfpb-acts-to-protect-the-public-from-black-box-credit-models-using-complex-algorithms/

5. Avivah Litan, Svetlana Sicular, Shubhangi Vashisth, Bern Elliot, and Farhan Choudhary, "Applying AI—Governance and Risk Management," *Gartner Research* (26 July 2021), ID G00745080.

6. Cynthia Rudin and Joanna Radin, "Why Are We Using Black Box Models in AI When We Don't Need To? A Lesson From An Explainable AI Competition," *Harvard Data Science Review*, 1(2) (2019), https://doi.org/10.1162/99608f92.5a8a3a3d

7. Jie Chen, Joel Vaughan, Vijayan N. Nair, and Agus Sudjianto, *Adaptive Explainable Neural Networks* (Cornell University: Arxiv, 2020), https://arxiv.org/abs/2004.02353v2

8. Marco Tulio Ribeiro, Sameer Singh, and Carlos Guestrin, ""Why Should I Trust You?": Explaining the Predictions of Any Classifier" *Proceedings of the 22nd ACM SIGKDD International Conference on Knowledge Discovery and Data Mining*, 1135–1144, San Francisco, California, USA.

9. Christoph Molnar, *Interpretable Machine Learning* (2021), https://christophm.github.io/interpretable-ml-book/

10. Adam White and Artur d'Avila Garcez, *Measurable Counterfactual Local Explanations for Any Classifier* (Cornell University, Arvix, 2019), https://arxiv.org/abs/1908.03020

11. Matt J. Kusner, Joshua R. Loftus, Chris Russell, and Ricardo Silva, *Counterfactual Fairness* (Cornell University, Arvix, 2017), https://arxiv.org/abs/1703.06856

12. Andreas C. Bueff, Mateusz Cytryński, Raffaella Calabrese, Matthew Jones, John Roberts, Jonathon Moore, Iain Brown, "Machine learning interpretability for a stress scenario generation in credit scoring based on counterfactuals," *Expert Systems with Applications* 202 (2022), 117271, ISSN 0957-4174, https://www.sciencedirect.com/science/article/pii/S0957417422006327

13. Riccardo Guidotti, Anna Monreale, Salvatore Ruggieri, Dino Pedreschi, Franco Turini, Fosca Giannotti, *Local Rule-Based Explanations of Black Box Decision Systems* (Cornell University, Arvix, 2018), https://arxiv.org/abs/1805.10820

14. Molnar, *Interpretable Machine Learning*.

15. Agus Sudjianto and Aijun Zhang, "Designing Inherently Interpretable Machine Learning Models," *New York, NY, USA, Proceedings of ACM ICAIF 2021 Workshop* (2021), https: //doi.org/10.1145/

16. Molnar, *Interpretable Machine Learning*.

CHAPTER 5

Bias, Fairness, and Vulnerability in Decision-Making

". . .you do not really understand a topic until you can teach it to a mechanical robot."

—Judea Pearl and Dana Mackenzie

In recent times, topics related to the ethical use of artificial intelligence (AI) and machine learning have been much debated by industry practitioners, regulators, and the public. It is now well understood that one of the unintended consequences of AI and machine learning is the risk of making biased decisions that can lead to unfair outcomes. The biases can stem from the historical and societal biases in the data that is used for training the models or introduced in the model development process itself. Biased models and decisions can lead to unintended consequences such as disparity or lack of access to the issuance of credit and insurance policies for minority groups.

One of the promises of AI and machine learning is to reduce bias and unfairness in financial decision-making, facilitated through automation. However, despite the promise, we do not need to look far to find examples where AI and machine learning reinforced bias and amplified unfairness in decision-making: from prioritizing job applications based on gender, to computer vision that discriminates based on race, to credit limit approvals that are gender biased.[1]

Data input and data capture by people, source systems, and applications that vary across different geographic localities can result in inaccuracies due to mislabeling, misinterpretation, or incomplete data processing. The data may not be representative of the population that the data will be applied on.

When the dataset used for model development includes historically biased outcomes, the same biased dataset is then used to train potentially biased models. In AI and machine learning, the issues that lead to bias increase the risk of unfair decisions and are made worse when characteristics or features that are correlated to protected variables are used. Protected variables are variables with legal or ethical restrictions. These can include groups that cannot be discriminated against in certain jurisdictions (e.g., demographic variables like gender and race). The models and business rules may also introduce bias.

It is also important to consider that bias in decision-making can originate from a range of sources, not only the training data. These sources may include the data used for model development, model assumptions, the models themselves, or business rules or other decisions made independently from the model that are impacting the model outcome.

Risk decisions are often further complicated by manual assessment processes and procedures where outcomes are by nature qualitative. An example includes judgmental decisions made by different manual assessors, analysts, and managers. Although most organizations have policies and procedures in place to guard against irresponsible conduct and hold decision makers accountable, it does not mean that all decisions are fully exempt from bias.

ASSESSING BIAS IN AI SYSTEMS

In recent years, the conversation of responsible AI has evolved from the philosophy of ethics in the use of machine-led decision-making, to a sociotechnological discussion on quantifiable ways to ensure automated systems are upheld by the same codes of conduct and ethical standards as human decision-making.

Keep in mind that with supervised learning, like AI and machine learning, predictive modeling is discriminatory by design, as the goal is to differentiate based on the values of a labeled variable. However, when the algorithm discriminates based on data that is nonrepresentative of the population or inputs with legal and ethical restrictions, it may violate consumer protection and data privacy laws. In the context of lending and insurance decisions, it is generally in the best interests of the services provider that the model outcome is as accurate as possible using all reasonably available information. This may come at the expense of the desire of the consumer, which is interested in the most favorable model outcome. This means that a careful balance is needed between business aims and fair and responsible model outcomes. Addressing bias and ensuring that decisions are made equitably can help safeguard vulnerable consumers from exploitation throughout their lifetime. To counter bias, fairness assessments should be embedded across the customer lifecycle (Figure 5.1). In this diagram, models at the point of loan onboarding have been selected as the working example, but assessing the fairness of outcomes is needful for model

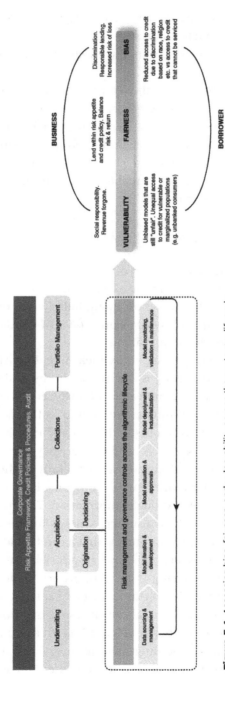

Figure 5.1 Assessing bias, fairness, and vulnerability across the customer lifecycle.

types across the customer lifecycle, including those used for account management and collection strategies.

For example, biased decisions at the time of onboarding, either from the model design or data capture, can result in measurable differences in the treatment of consumers with similar risk profiles, and are considered unfair.

Fairness is concerned with the fair decisions of models and the equitable distribution of benefits. Consumers' vulnerability is measured along the customer journey and is typically marked by circumstantial changes that can be worsened by unfair decisions. For services providers, it is becoming increasingly important to incorporate the vulnerability of consumers in their decision-making. For example, a change in circumstances can lead to financial stress and may require active account management.

Importantly, balancing fairness with business objectives will require:

- Assessing a range of fairness metrics to mitigate different types of bias (data bias, model bias, evaluation bias, etc.), including an ability to select metrics appropriate to the context in which the model is used
- Ensuring that fairness assessments are embedded in the end-to-end model lifecycle and decisioning processes
- Using powerful tools to assess fairness at an individual and group level

The use of advanced fairness measurement tools supports the careful analysis of protected variables, the investigation of fairness risk, and its root causes.

In this chapter, we explain the current definitions and measures of bias, fairness, and vulnerability as they relate to data and models. It must be noted that most risk models, whether traditional, statistical models, or those developed using AI and machine learning, need to be assessed for latent bias and unfairness. With AI and machine learning, bias and unfairness are more challenging to detect by human intuition alone. In this chapter, we focus on the application of models as it relates to impacting consumers. That does not preclude other types of models from the risk of leading to unfair decisions. Having said that, this chapter will pay attention to vulnerability concerns throughout the customer journey. This will be helpful to ensure that automated systems are able to deliver on the promise of addressing fairness in decision-making and thus increasing the value of the risk models to organizations, consumers, and society.

WHAT IS BIAS?

Bias in AI systems occurs when human prejudice based on mistaken assumptions becomes part of the way automated decisions are made. A well-intentioned algorithm may inadvertently make biased decisions that may discriminate against or treat protected groups of consumers differently.

Bias may occur and enter at any point in the model lifecycle. A common misnomer is that bias stems only from training data that is not well diversified, and although that is a common source for bias to arise in automated systems, in fact, bias may enter the model lifecycle much earlier—for example, in the way the problem statement is formulated or in the way data gets collected.

When the bias stays undetected, it may be systematized and amplified by automated decision systems.

In risk models—including those leveraging AI and machine learning—bias may stem from the training data. Such issues may arise from historical biases as well as the ways in which the data is sampled, collected, and processed. This means that the training data is not representing the population to which the model will be applied, leading to unfair decisions. Bias can also be created during the model design phase. That can create measurable differences in the way a model performs in definable subpopulations based on a profile. For example, the profile can be based on the variables included or approximated in model construction like age, gender, race, ethnicity, and religion. An example is the historical racial bias that has been captured by credit bureau scores. Although the scores are not capturing race directly, they have been developed on historical data that includes payment history, amounts owed, length of credit history, new credit, and credit mix information. These variables are themselves influenced by the generational wealth that African American and Hispanic borrowers did not have equal access to. This bias will continue to produce lower credit scores and lower ability to access credit for these groups.[2] As another example, in 2015, the White House together with the Federal Trade Commission conducted research that found that as consumers operate in groups, minority groups may be unfairly treated when big data is used for credit scoring. The study emphasized the need to assess correlations of key drivers with protected variables when big data is used.[3]

WHAT IS FAIRNESS?

Fairness is considered a moral primitive and is by nature judgmental. Given its qualitative character, it is more challenging to define fairness comprehensively and globally across applications. Distinct cultures will have different definitions of what constitutes a fair decision. The philosophy of fairness is outside the scope of the book; however, when it comes to the technological approaches to incorporate fairness checks in AI systems, in recent years, system integrators and software providers have started to package fairness detection and remediation techniques.

Most societies uphold values of equality and equity. In the USA, fair lending laws, such as Regulation B and the Equal Credit Opportunity Act (ECOA), protect consumers from discrimination in lending decisions. The statute makes it unlawful for any creditor to discriminate against any applicant with respect to any aspect of a credit transaction based on race, color, religion, national origin, sex, marital status, or age.

Any adverse action for credit needs to be supported by evidence to prove the decision is not based on a prohibited characteristic. The Consumer Financial Protection Bureau has recently published a report with guidelines on the use of AI-based lending decisions.[4] In summary, it emphasizes the need for explanations that can help lenders generate fair lending and adverse action notices, while utilizing AI and machine learning models.

In the context of algorithmic models, the widespread practice is to associate fairness with equitable decisions and parity in the distribution of benefits across demographic segments.

Kusner, Russell, and Silva[5] define algorithms as fair on a range of fairness levels. For example, if an algorithm is fair through unawareness, then the algorithm is unaware of protected variables, and therefore cannot discriminate against groups of protected variables.

An unintended consequence of fairness through unawareness is that a combination of characteristics may inadvertently approximate protected variables.

Kusner et al. go further in defining a second level of fairness when an algorithm gives similar predictions to similar consumers. In addition, a third level of fairness is seen when the algorithm supplies equality of opportunity and similarity across demographics. Finally, a fourth level of fairness is observed when an algorithm is counterfactually fair—that is, fair in the actual dimension, as well as in the counterfactual dimension.

A problem with fairness is that when fairness expectations are translated into quantifiable terms, these terms are not mutually exclusive. A recidivism example highlighted the nonexclusivity of fairness metrics.[6]

TYPES OF BIAS IN DECISION-MAKING

Bias may stem from multiple sources. Let us differentiate between cognitive and statistical biases.

In the early 1970s, Amos Tversky and Daniel Kahneman[7] introduced the term *cognitive biases* to describe people's systematic but purportedly flawed patterns of responses to decision problems.

When putting in place a governance framework for AI and machine learning, it is helpful to first consider the types of cognitive bias to be aware of, and the controls that can safeguard against these.

A few of the cognitive biases are:[8]

- Overconfidence results from a false sense of control, optimism, and the desirability effect: an AI system will make fair predictions because we want it to. A variant of that is the herd mentality (see below).
- Self-serving bias results from a human tendency to attribute good success to skills and bad success to unfortunate events: an AI system is correct on a set of data because the model is well developed, and inaccurate on another, not due to poor construction, but population drift or other uncontrollable reasons.
- Herd mentality is when decision-making is performed by blindly copying what peers are doing. In this case, the decision

is influenced by heuristic simplification or emotion rather than independent analysis.

- Loss aversion is a tendency to experience larger regret from losing than satisfaction from winning.
- Framing is when a decision is made based on the way the information has been represented. If it was represented in another way, a different conclusion would be reached.
- Narrative bias is a human tendency to make sense of the world using stories. Information that does not fit the storyline gets ignored.
- Anchoring occurs when preexisting data is used as reference point and influences later decisions.
- Confirmation bias is a tendency to seek out information and data to confirm preexisting ideas.
- Representativeness heuristic is a false sense that if two objects are similar, they are also correlated.

Here are some common sources of statistical bias:

- Selection bias occurs when the data for model development is systemically different from the population to which the model will be applied.
- Sampling bias refers to an error caused by non-random sampling. It means that the data will not be representative of the population. It can occur based on the data collection method, confirmation bias, the selected time interval or changes made to the raw data.
- Survivorship bias is a variant of selection bias, the phenomenon where only those who "survived" a lengthy process are included in or excluded from the analysis, thus creating a biased sample.

Current Guidance, Laws, and Regulations

As there is, in general, a lack of legislation on fairness in AI systems, a good example to consider is of existing consumer protection frameworks. As mentioned in the previous section, the Fair Credit Reporting

Act and the Equal Credit Opportunity Act (ECOA) defined the standards for fair lending in the United States.

The Fair Credit Reporting Act (Title VI of the Consumer Credit Protection Act) enforces the protection of consumer data and limits its use to specific purposes as specified by the act. It also allows for the investigation of disputed information.

The Equal Credit Opportunity Act (Regulation B) promotes equal access to credit to creditworthy applicants and prohibits discrimination based on race, skin color, religion, national origin, sex, marital status, or age. It goes further to notify applicants of actions taken on their application, to collect information on race for dwelling-related loans, and to keep records of applications.

Even though fair lending in credit decisions has been regulated in some jurisdictions for decades, there are still persistent issues with the fair treatment of minority groups and equal access to credit.

Having said that, we do have a precedent of how fairness in some automated systems is regulated today, together with industry consultation on how that can be extended for AI and machine learning.

Given its evolving nature, the intention of the next section is not to present a final solution to address fairness (and bias) in automated systems, but to provide an overview of current and evolving practices.

Methods and Measures to Address Bias and Fairness

Many measures have been developed in different areas, such as finance, insurance, and healthcare, to identify bias in data and to assess the fairness of model outcomes. For risk management, it is recommended that bias and fairness measures are embedded as controls throughout the lifecycle of the customer and across the risk model lifecycle (Figure 5.1). It is important to understand the limitations of fairness metrics: the measures to detect bias and fairness cannot guarantee the presence or absence of bias and fairness or expunge the fact that fairness concerns can appear later due to other exogenous factors, such as changes to data. Next, we will explain some of the methods and measures that can be used to detect and remediate bias by signaling for human intervention to correct bias and fairness issues.

At the time of writing, the development of fairness metrics is maturing, including metrics for AI and machine learning.

Following are examples of common approaches and metrics used to detect bias and fairness:

1. **Demographic parity.** This is where each segment of a demographic variable, or "protected class," is assessed to receive the same positive outcome at an equal rate.

2. **Equal opportunity.** The metric validates that the true positive rate between segments is the same. By extension, it also measures that an equal true negative rate is observed across segments.

3. **False positive rate balance.** It measures that the false positive rates (and by virtue, the true negative rates) between segments are equal. An example is loan applicants, where the rate balance ensures a representative fraction of each segment that is predicted to default on their loan.

4. **Equalized odds or average odds.** This assumes that the true positive rates between segments and the false positive rates between segments are equal (equivalently, equal true negative rates and equal false negative rates).

5. **Positive predictive parity.** Here, the positive predictive value between segments is equal (i.e., each segment has the same false negative predictive rates). This is achieved by comparing the fraction of true positives to the fraction of predicted positives in each segment.

6. **False omission rate balance.** The false omission rates between segments are equal (i.e., the segments have equal negative predictive value). The rate compares the fraction of false negatives to the fraction of rejections/negative benefit.

7. **Feature attribution analysis.** Utilize feature attribution analysis to find drivers that affect decisions, for example, to ensure that factors are not correlated with protected variables.

8. **Sensitivity analysis.** Perturbations are used to assess sensitivity to changes in demographics.

9. **Correlation analysis.** When there are variables that are correlated with sensitive variables such as age, sex, or family status, it can lead to unfair outcomes.

10. **Cross referencing.** Utilize outcome analysis and cross-referencing to assess model accuracy across protected and nonprotected groups. An unfair individual decision may be observable in a particular demographic segment but is not measurable when the entire population is considered.

11. **Triangulation.** This is where a situation is explored in depth using more than two sources to validate findings. There are other types of triangulations:

   - *Methodology:* using more than one method to gather data points and where more than one measure is used.
   - *Data:* involving varying dimensions such as time, space, and person.
   - *Investigator:* where more than one person is involved.

12. **Counterfactual analysis.** To assess fairness at the individual level, in counterfactual analysis, to evaluate the change in outcome, the causal attributes of the same record is compared with an adjusted version of the record.

As mentioned previously, a good starting point is to assess for bias and fairness by comparing the prediction and performance made by a model for different values of protected or "sensitive" variables (Figure 5.2). Examples of sensitive variables are those that are demographic in nature, including variables such as age, gender, race, religion, family status, marital status, and ethnicity.

Using AI and Machine Learning to Detect and Remediate Bias: A Word of Caution

In some cases, the use of AI and machine learning can help detect and remediate bias automatically. Similar to other AI and machine learning use cases, to assess fair lending risk may pose the same challenges of explainability (understanding the reason for a prediction estimate). One of the challenges to confirming AI-based models is that

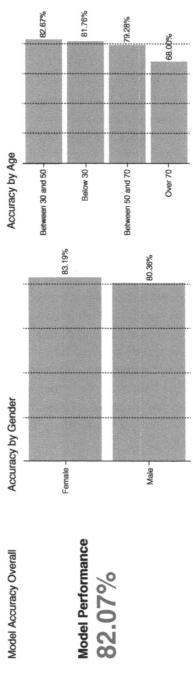

Figure 5.2 Disparity analyses assess model performance across classes of protected characteristics (in this case, gender and age).

some traditional model validation approaches or metrics are not readily applicable. The drivers behind the decisions cannot be easily found or separated from other variables due to the additional complexity of the input data and algorithms.

Another challenge is to understand why the AI and machine learning identified a high risk of bias given its inherent inability to justify the inclusion of model variables, compared to a traditional, statistical model where the variables and signs of parameters are known.

The AI system itself may be subject to protected variables implicitly or indirectly. In this case, standard techniques to determine correlations in the model can be applied. In addition, explainability metrics can be used to explain the main drivers behind decisions. Model sensitivity analysis, benchmarking, and trade-off analysis are other popular methods that are often used by financial institutions to test and confirm models.

In summary, AI approaches will still need to follow existing consumer protection and regulatory frameworks (including Regulation B and the ECOA). Like any other type of model, AI models can be flawed and are also subject to bias, which impacts model predictability. Bias can be caused by either data or algorithms that cause the model to be insufficiently or incorrectly trained. When the sample data used to train the models does not sufficiently represent the population, the model that will be applied to over- or underrepresenting minority groups will have higher risk of unfair treatment. If the AI is biased, that bias will be perpetuated and potentially be amplified through automated decision-making.

A benefit of automation is that if the bias is properly addressed, automated decision-making has the potential to be more consistent and traceable than human decision-making. In areas with strict requirements for explainability, model governance frameworks should be extended with the specifics for AI and machine learning.

Model risks associated with AI-based modeling approaches can be more pronounced as complex algorithms and input data are usually involved in the modeling process. Complex transformations or interdependence of model variables can make it more challenging to uncover hidden patterns that may potentially violate fair lending laws. Thus, it is more important for institutions to ensure model risk management principles and governance are enforced when developing AI and machine learning.

These principles aid the evaluation of AI-based approaches as many organizations have in place model risk and data governance systems.

Financial institutions must prove their understanding of the model inaccuracies and potential for unintended consequences (i.e., risk of noncompliance with fair lending laws).

Robust model risk management framework will collect, and make readily available, information that consistently and reliably enforces fair lending laws. This can be further extended to financial institutions having the ability to recognize and remediate the potential for discrimination above and beyond regulations.

In addition, financial institutions can enforce constraints or rules on input data, ensure that the training data does not have protected characteristics, apply data quality checks to prevent data measures from contamination or influence by subjective errors, and document and validate the methods used to debias the data.

Vulnerability

Today, the identification of customers that are "vulnerable" is not regulated in all given authorities. Despite this, understanding that customers are more vulnerable to disruption in the customer lifecycle by unfair decisions, or changes that impact lifestyle is a key consideration by market players that issue products and services. These lifecycles have many stages, ranging from the point of awareness or investigation through to an expanding relationship where more products or services are acquired by a customer, including, financial services (including unregulated "fringe" lenders), insurance, superannuation, and telecommunications (Figure 5.3).

As a customer journey with a market player progresses from awareness through to expanding the existing relationship the risk to vulnerability "shocks" can increase. There are many different contact channels that exist between a market player and a customer that can serve as interaction points to assess the increased likelihood of customer vulnerability.

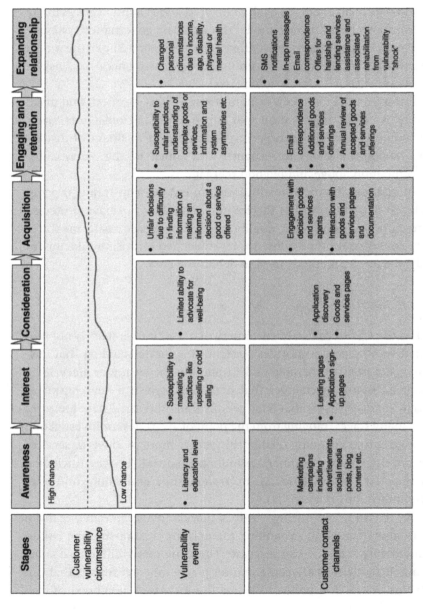

Figure 5.3 Vulnerability is a key consideration that market players that offer products, goods, and services are starting to consider throughout their entire journey with customers.

Protecting vulnerable customers from hardship or stress has continued to be a major consideration throughout the COVID-19 pandemic and left many small business owners facing serious financial stress and insolvency. The stress has shown to also extend to homeownership, where mortgagees have changed their repayments or deferred them. For financial credit providers, there is value in predicting which customers are more likely to default after the expiration of a repayment deferral program. Such models focus on the major stress event of a pandemic, but not on the increased risk of vulnerability that may have existed before the COVID-19 pandemic. Such latent vulnerability risk is important to understand and model, especially considering the best opportunity to provide support through the customer journey (Figure 5.3).

Regulators are increasingly focusing their attention on better understanding the context in which automated decision systems operate. Better protecting vulnerable customers has been receiving attention from the government and regulatory bodies long before the COVID-19 pandemic but has become more pronounced in recent times.

For example, the energy regulator in the United Kingdom, Office of Gas and Electricity markets (OFGEM), published its first consumer vulnerability strategy in 2013.[9] The strategy helped OFGEM to better understand vulnerable consumers, which in turn led to the development of frameworks and the practical implementation of consumer protection policies for better decision-making.

For consumer lending, the Financial Conduct Authority (also in the United Kingdom) has a broad definition for vulnerable consumers as "...someone who, due to their personal circumstances, is especially susceptible to detriment, particularly when a firm is not acting with appropriate level of care."

Their guidance defines the details on the key drivers and characteristics of vulnerability. Key drivers include health, financial ability, financial resiliency, and life events.

The FCA defines the personal, behavioral, social, and market-led characteristics that may be associated with increased vulnerability of consumers as:

- Age—young or old
- Living in a remote area
- Low income
- Periods of over-indebtedness
- Homelessness
- Having an indigenous background
- Low reading, writing, and numerical skills
- Speaking a primary language other than the predominant language of a country
- Diverse cultural background, assumptions, or attitudes
- Having either an intellectual, psychiatric, physical, sensory, neurological, or learning disability
- Having limited access to technology
- Inexperience with products or services offered
- Insufficient or misleading information released to the market

The FCA published guidance as well as policies like Policy 18/19 that highlights the importance of assessing affordability in credit risk, including the use of income and expenditure information. In 2017, the FCA published guidance on conduct for forbearance that helps guide financial institutions on how to better embed fairness and assessments of the customer's ability to repay into their pre-collections and collections treatment strategies.

By better understanding vulnerable consumers, financial institutions can offer better services, reduce losses, and avoid costly investigations into misconduct. This can be achieved by:

- Making better use of internal demographic data so that vulnerable customers are better identified
- Developing toolkits or using third-party software to help design frameworks, governance processes, and products and services to reduce vulnerability
- Engaging with customers at the earliest time possible to help with the design of products and services to mitigate the impacts of vulnerability

■ Tailoring offerings of products and services to ensure appropriateness for vulnerable customers

The costs of not investing in better identifying or protecting vulnerable customers are high. This can involve multi-million-dollar penalties imposed due to the violation of consumer protection laws as well as reputational damage. On the other side, implementing vulnerability safeguards can generate benefits such as better customer and employee satisfaction and improved sales opportunities from more flexible products and services for a wider range of customers.

At financial institutions, the efforts underway are often driven by regulatory compliance. An example is reducing the time needed to resolve customer-initiated disputes. Some of the early studies have leveraged sentiment analysis using voice-to-text data to find sequences of sentiments that are expressed during a discussion. These sequences are then used as classifiers to predict dispute or nondispute targets.[10] Furthermore, convolutional neural networks can also be applied to voice-to-text data to identify sentiment word vectors.[11] Dispute resolution and complaints analysis represents an easy way to apply advanced analytics to reduce the time to resolution and scale across multiple interaction channels across the enterprise.

CONCLUDING REMARKS

The use of advanced analytics to better understand bias, fairness, and the vulnerability of consumers is increasingly being brought to the frontline, rather than functioning in the back or middle office. Creating frameworks and processes to mitigate bias and assess fairness in decision-making will mean that in future these can also be expanded to other risk models, including those used for real-time risk assessments, and the managing and mitigation of emerging risks.

ENDNOTES

1. Basileal Imana, Aleksandra Korolova, and John Heidemann, "Auditing for discrimination in algorithms delivering job ads." In *Proceedings of The Web Conference 2021* (WWW '21), Ljubljana, Slovenia, (April 19–23, 2021), https://ant.isi.edu/datasets/addelivery/; Larry Hardesty, "Study finds gender and skin-type bias in commercial artificial-intelligence systems," *MIT News* (February 11, 2018), https://news.mit

.edu/2018/study-finds-gender-skin-type-bias-artificial-intelligence-systems-0212; Associated Press, NY regulator investigating Apple Card for possible gender bias. *NBC News* (November 10, 2019), https://www.nbcnews.com/tech/apple/ny-regulator-investigating-apple-card-possible-gender-bias-n1079581

2. N. Campisi, *From Inherent Racial Bias to Incorrect Data—The Problems with Current Credit Scoring Models* (Los Angeles: Forbes Advisor, 2021).

3. The World Bank, *Financial Consumer Protection and New forms of data processing beyond credit reporting* (2018) https://elibrary.worldbank.org/doi/abs/10.1596/31009

4. Bureau of Consumer Financial Protection, *Fair Lending Report of the Bureau of Consumer Financial Protection* (2020), https://files.consumerfinance.gov/f/documents/cfpb_2019-fair-lending_report.pdf

5. Matt J. Kusner, Joshua R. Loftus, Chris Russell, and Ricardo Silva, "*Counterfactual fairness,*" *arXiv* 1703(06856) (2017), 1–18.

6. Sam Corbett-Davies, Emma Pierson, Avi Feller, and Sharad Goel, "A computer program used for bail and sentencing decisions was labeled biased against blacks. It's actually not that clear," *Washington Post* (2016), https://www.washingtonpost.com/news/monkey-cage/wp/2016/10/17/can-an-algorithm-be-racist-our-analysis-is-more-cautious-than-propublicas/

7. Amos Tversky and Daniel Kahneman, "Judgment under uncertainty: Heuristics and biases: Biases in judgments reveal some heuristics of thinking under uncertainty, *Science* 185(4157) (1974): 1124–1131.

8. Marcus Lu, "50 cognitive biases in the modern world," *Visual Capitalist* (February 1, 2020), https://www.visualcapitalist.com/50-cognitive-biases-in-the-modern-world/

9. Kate Smith, *Consumer Vulnerability Strategy* (London: Ofgem, 2013), https://www.ofgem.gov.uk/sites/default/files/docs/2013/07/consumer-vulnerability-strategy_0.pdf

10. Lu Wang and Claire Cardie, *A Piece of My Mind: A Sentiment Analysis Approach* (Ithaca, NY: arXiv.org, 2016).

11. Man Lan, Zhihua Zhang, Yue Lu, and Ju Wu, *Three Convolutional Neural Network-based Models for Learning Sentiment Word Vectors towards Sentiment Analysis* (Vancouver, BC:, International Joint Conference on Neural Networks (IJCNN), 2016).

CHAPTER 6

Machine Learning Model Deployment, Implementation, and Making Decisions

As we have established in previous chapters, a step change in the use of AI, machine learning, and automation in risk and compliance functions, the question is not whether it has transformational potential—that's a given—but rather how to better operationalize AI and machine learning in an ethical, responsible, and sustainable way.

The opportunities that these innovative models present are broad: it is said to give better accuracy in the quantification of risk, deeper insights into big data, and efficiency gains from the automation of repetitive tasks.

AI and machine learning only deliver value when organizations take actions based on the insights. Regardless of how impressive an AI or machine learning looks in the laboratory, it is only when the AI is deployed in the real world that it delivers tangible benefit to impact the bottom line.

With the increased sophistication in algorithms, deployments are an increasingly challenging hurdle organizations are facing. Many of these modern models do not make it into production. According to a Gartner report in 2021, only 53% of POC (proof of concept) models made it beyond the lab to production systems, and this process still took on average 9 months.[1] Similarly, research from SAS indicates that only half of AI models built make it to production. In other words, only half of developed models end up generating business value, and often these models take too long before they are fully operational—further eroding their impacts in decision-making.

One reason for the small number of AI and machine learning in production today is the limitations associated with legacy environments. By design, these systems were not set up for newer AI and machine learning.

Many organizations have established processes associated with their legacy environments. Although incumbent, legacy systems have reached a workable level of operation for existing models, these are not without their own challenges—as explained in the next section. One reason for slow deployments is that historically, the development and deployment of risk models occurred in systems that are both physically and logically separate. Different systems that are in use for development and production typically have different cadences for updates, and often different programming languages.

The inability to deploy AI and machine learning at scale has started to create bottlenecks across the analytical value chain. The business value that AI and machine learning can generate from contributing to decisions in a production environment cannot materialize as the models are trapped as data science projects. It erodes the "wow" effect of newer and more sophisticated models.

The good news is that the technologies for model deployment have also advanced in recent years.

A major driver for innovation in this area is enterprise digital transformation. It has radically changed the way in which organizations, including financial services, engage with their customers and other stakeholders. To meet expectations for hyperpersonalized and always-on services, decision-making is becoming more digital, relevant, and real-time. In general, the goals of digital transformation efforts are not only to provide a digital channel but also to improve operational efficiency, agility, and speed to bring new digital services and products to market.

The technologies underpinning model deployment have taken strides from the manual recoding of model logic, to where AI and machine learning can now integrate into existing services and front-end applications, either directly or via application programming interfaces (APIs). An API allows the model to be called as a service via an API endpoint. Models can also be directly deployed to containers or other run-time environments.

TYPICAL MODEL DEPLOYMENT CHALLENGES

As mentioned, a key driver for innovation is the organization's digital transformation objectives. A global trend is for financial services to modernize their technological infrastructure by combining on-premises and cloud-based architectures, resulting in a much open ecosystem and closer cooperation between developers and operations. For example, modern infrastructures have evolved from physical servers to cloud-based or hybrid architectures, which is a combination of on-premises environments and the public cloud. Also, the development process and management of new applications have evolved from a traditional waterfall approach to agile approaches, while the deployment of major updates has progressed from occasional upgrades (once or twice yearly) to software applications that follow a continuous integration/ continuous development paradigm for deployment of updates.

It is in this environment, with a greater degree of distribution and complexity, that modern risk models are developed, deployed, and maintained in production.

These bottlenecks in having a streamlined and automated deployment in place are not limited to AI and machine learning—these apply to traditional, statistical models too, but given their complexity and self-learning characteristics, deployment challenges are often exacerbated with the use of AI and machine learning. With that in mind, let us review the key challenges in model deployment that organizations face.

Lack of Structured Deployment Processes

Analytical projects are often conducted in silos within most organizations—a reflection of how data is organized according to each internal department. This has led to the formation of fragmented analytics initiatives and capabilities. It also means that the governance and structuring of analytical initiatives is left to the responsibility of each department in turn, leading to longer model deployment cycles, without having a standardized enterprise-wide approach for analytical projects.

Another hurdle is the separation between development and deployment environments. In some instances, organizations have adopted an experimental approach to analytics, which means that the model development is done in an ad-hoc way, rather than following a standardized process that is designed for a simplified deployment in production. Often, models are prevented from successful deployment due to the incorrect specification of the model logic, the input data, or limitations in operating systems (e.g., some production systems cannot handle nonlinear transformations).

Many organizations are actively seeking technological capabilities, which help centralize model development and deployment processes. The SAS platform introduces this capability by allowing organizations to define and track custom workflows for model lifecycle management. Figure 6.1 is an example of how the end-to-end process can be

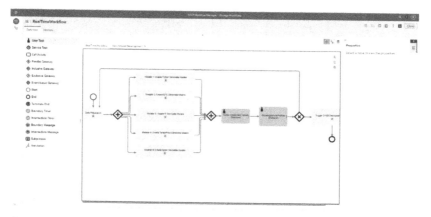

Figure 6.1 A simplified workflow for model lifecycle management.

structured in a series of tasks for developing, validating, and approving a model.

The Need to Manually Recode Complex Models

As mentioned above, as models are typically developed in siloes, it requires translation of the model logic from one application system to another. Taking a hypothetical example, the back office may use a custom software application for statistical modeling to develop a new loss forecasting model. This model will need to be applied during a regular monthly impairment calculation process, as well as in a front office system for the pricing of new commercial loans. This will require the translation of the model logic into the system used for monthly impairment calculations, as well as into the front office system used by credit analysts as they structure new deals. This is a challenge as it increases the operational model risk (e.g., potential for coding error in translation resulting in incorrect impairment values), delays in the model delivering value to the organization (as it takes time to recode the new model), and a lack of flexibility to make changes to the model in the event of a required model change.

With consistently packaged algorithmic code and data that follows a "build once, deploy anywhere" approach, inefficient, repetitive, and manual deployment tasks can be avoided (Figure 6.2). In addition, it improves the scalability and agility of model deployments.

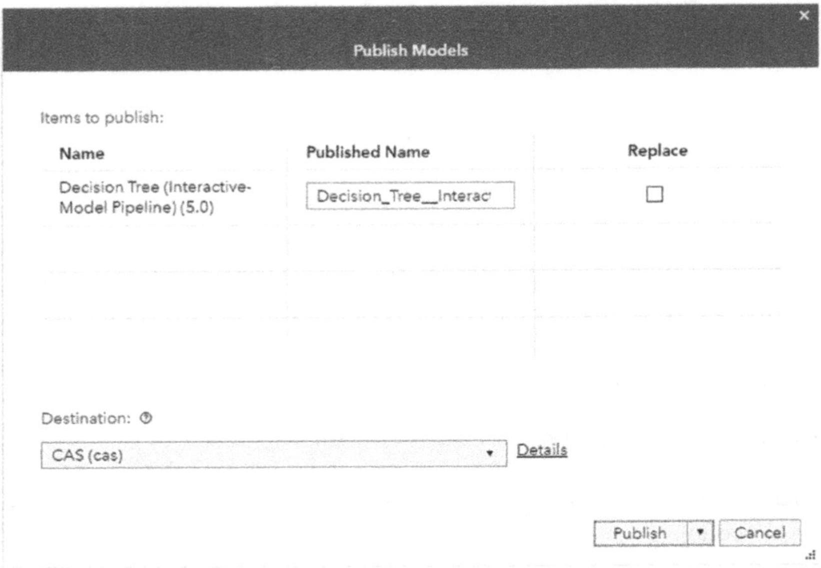

Figure 6.2 Direct deployment to a batch process.

Managing Multiple Analytical Tools and Programming Languages

In recent years, with the rapid development of open-source technologies, risk modelers have more flexibility and access to a range of modeling techniques, combined with support from open community forums. For the IT (information technology) departments, responsible for managing the deployment of new risk models, it requires knowledge of a range of different programming languages. A single deployment approach, regardless of model development language, that follows the same standardized process (Figure 6.3) for a range of risk models provides flexibility to model developers in their preferences of programming language.

Signoff and Approvals

To productionize new risk models, proper signoffs, documentation, and approvals from internal and sometimes external stakeholders are needed. To include a new model in a "live" production system may

Figure 6.3 Standardized model development and deployment process.

require additional technical approvals and documentation. The model deployment and the ongoing maintenance of a model in a production system are subject to the governance framework, including having the necessary model contingency plans in place.

Adoption of Agile Practices for ModelOps

Success and proficiency in the use of agile practices in developing and deploying software has led to the increased adoption of these practices for developing and deploying analytical models as well. Crucial to enabling agile practices is the use of the appropriate technology for an organization's specific needs. The right technology enables efficient and reliable deployment of software, fast feedback for improvement, and enables greater experimentation to test new ideas—all of which are key goals of an agile method.

Similarly, organizations are looking to achieve the same goals for analytical models. However, analytical models are more than just code—they are data dependent, have precise monitoring requirements, and are used to drive key business decisions. It is because of these distinctions that there is a challenge in taking only an IT-led agile approach, where tools designed to be effective for software development are ineffective for analytical models. Therefore, for an organization to adopt agile practices for models, also known as ModelOps, it must be able to design a process that includes appropriate analytical tools that can integrate with its existing successful agile software development practices.

DEPLOYMENT SCENARIOS

The decision on how to deploy a model is determined by how the outputs of the model are consumed. The choice of deployment scenario involves a distinct set of infrastructural requirements for the processing of the models within the context of how the model outcomes will be used. Typically, these resemble the following types of scenarios.

Deploying Models in Batch Processes

Batch processing (Figure 6.2) is a common way to deploy many risk models. Large volumes of data that are collated over a period can be processed in batch when convenient. This method is a highly efficient way to score models for use cases that are not time sensitive. Typically, the infrastructures required for batch deployments are simpler than those required for real-time deployments. For example, to perform monthly scoring for limit increase approvals, a process will extract data from source systems and apply the data transformation, model scoring, and other post-processing logic to calculate the model output, including the pre-approved limits. One of the main benefits of batch processing is that compute resources can be planned for. It can be made available for regular processing or scheduled to run off-peak:

- Generate model output for business decisions that are not time sensitive.
- Data inputs that are accumulated over a period before models are scored.

Deploying Models in Real Time

In today's world, society has grown used to services and systems that respond instantaneously. In this scenario, model outputs are time sensitive, often with the expectation to be available on demand.

Financial institutions are increasingly competing in supplying services and risk decisions instantly. In such a scenario, risk models must be deployed in real time. For example, for new loan approvals, the risk assessment of a customer based on the input data gets generated immediately on request to decide to approve or reject the application.

Another example is in fraud detection and prevention. Financial institutions often have in place fraud detection models that were developed on historical cases of suspicious transactions. These systems score each new transaction based on a combination of customer and transaction information to find suspicious activity. As the goal is to stop a fraudulent transaction from being processed, these models need to supply answers in real time:

- Model outputs for business decisions are time sensitive.
- Model outputs are generated at the transactional level.
- Model output rates must be as close as possible to data input rates.

Modern infrastructures are evolving where we see variations to the deployment of models to batch or real-time applications.

In some instances, mostly for batch deployments, the model logic can be deployed to execute within a database, reducing the need for data movement, and increasing the speed and efficiency of the scoring process.

Financial institutions are also increasingly adopting a cloud-based, microservices architecture where models are deployed as analytic services in containers. In this way, models are deployed in the cloud as lightweight as possible. The container software manages the operating layer and is accessed easily through an API endpoint. This option supports both batch and real-time deployment scenarios.

We next explain three deployment options for risk models: in-database deployment, to lightweight containers, or directly in business decision workflows.

Deployment of Models in Database Management Systems

With the explosion of data, big datasets are typically stored in database management systems. To reduce the need for data movement, modern technologies enable the deployment of data preparation, model logic, and decision logic to where the data is residing, rather than moving the data to a compute environment for processing. The benefits are reduced input/output to transfer the data between systems, better performance, and a smaller memory footprint needed for analytical processing.

Deployment of Models to Lightweight Containers

Models can also be deployed as lightweight containers. In this case and in general, the container is exposed by an API to allow it to be accessed from anywhere within a wider ecosystem. With the progressive adoption of software applications being deployed as containers, this approach has been adopted for models as well—it being particularly effective for open-source models, as running in a container allows for easier management of the packages and dependencies of the models.

Putting models into containers makes it ideal for an organization to run efficient analytical workloads in the cloud. Models deployed in containers allow an organization to flexibly scale the infrastructure for running models, as per their business needs. Model container deployment can suit both batch and real-time paradigms, as containers can be scaled to meet computational requirements—for example, every month (batch) or as more users are requesting model output from a live web application (real time).

Additionally, within a cloud-based architecture, containerizing models can greatly ease the integration of models with other applications. Models as containers are managed by the same container orchestration tools and CI/CD infrastructure as other software applications, essentially managing them as analytical microservices.

Deployments in Business Decision Workflows

The output of models can take on the form of predicted probabilities or predicted numerical values. While informative, these results often need to be integrated with business rules to deliver business-specific outcomes (Figure 6.4).

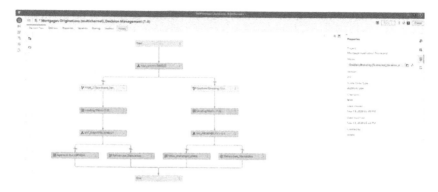

Figure 6.4 Deployment of models to decision strategies.

In the case for fraud detection, in isolation, the fraud model would produce a predicted probability of a transaction being fraudulent. However, there needs to be an integration with post-processing decision logic. An example of that could be a combination of the transaction amount and the fraud probability to compute an expected fraud amount. The expected fraud amount can help in prioritizing flagged transactions for investigation.

It is through the integration with decisioning workflows and business logic that the true business value can be extracted from analytical models. Organizations with the technological capability to automate the integration will realize the return on investment in AI and machine learning more efficiently.

CASE STUDY: ENTERPRISE DECISIONING AT A GLOBAL BANK

One of the largest banks in the world chose to strengthen their digital capability for the future. They wanted to offer their customers a seamless experience across business lines: credit risk, collections, and fraud detection. The platform supported their digital transformation objectives to offer consistent and contextual customer journeys. Furthermore, during the proof of value, it has improved the speed of credit decisions (straight-through-processing (STP) rates from 60 to 75%) while the deployment of new models, previously taking six months on average for their mortgage portfolio, can now be achieved in weeks. Similarly, the time it takes to deploy new machine learning models for their consumer loans portfolio has been reduced from weeks to days.

PRACTICAL CONSIDERATIONS

Begin with the End in Mind

In reviewing the risk model lifecycle as depicted in Chapter 3 and shown in Figure 6.5, each step affects the deployment of the model. For example, the first step in the process is the initiation of the model development project. First, it makes sense to ask, where will the model be deployed? And how will the model outputs be consumed? How often and how soon do users need the model outputs?

Second, the data preparation and transformations of the model will form part of the scoring logic. It makes sense to ask, what data sources will be needed to prepare the data and score the model?

Third, keep in mind, in general, that AI and machine learning algorithms require heavy compute power for development, but may be surprisingly light when it comes to scoring (e.g., neural networks for function approximation).

Furthermore, the post-modeling processes, including decision logic and the feedback for regular monitoring of the model, are all design decisions that will affect the ease of deployment. We next describe key considerations of regular, continuous model monitoring.

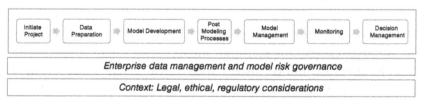

Figure 6.5 The steps in the risk model lifecycle within the context of legal, ethical, and regulatory constraints.

Continuous Model Monitoring

Traditionally, financial institutions have in place standard monitoring processes for risk models. Risk models are typically subject to regulatory compliance that requires regular performance tracking.

As the number of risk models are ever increasing, the sophistication of modeling methods deployed by financial institutions is also increasing. This is particularly clear with the adoption of AI and machine learning, where enhanced transparency is often needed. As new data becomes available, AI and machine learning are often dynamically updated, which requires that the performance of the model is monitored dynamically. Many metrics are tracked to ensure that the model is performing as expected, including data quality, model drift, explainability, model robustness, and bias.

By automatically and dynamically tracking the performance, including champion and challenger models, risk departments will be better equipped to proactively find issues that may lead to model failure (Figure 6.6).

MODEL ORCHESTRATION

How the lifecycle of a model is managed, especially after deployment, is crucial. If a model starts to drift, how long does it take to retrain on

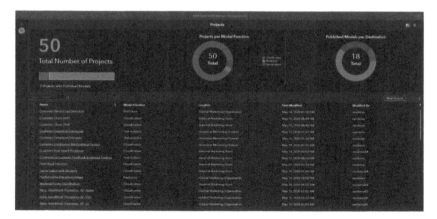

Figure 6.6 Continuous monitoring of models in production.

new data? If it needs to be replaced with a new champion, what steps need to be taken to implement a new model in production? Furthermore, with newer innovations and adopted technologies such as cloud and containers, integrating analytics as part of these systems requires a process that can carefully guide workflow from analytics platforms into other software and IT environments.

To ensure that the model lifecycle can be managed, it is important to have an orchestration layer that can enable both automation and governance. Automation is key to enabling speed, whether it's ensuring that models can be re-trained, or deployed as quickly as possible, or even implementing into business rules. At the same time, governance is paramount to ensure that the correct approvals are made by the correct stakeholders. By enabling approval and user input, organizations ensure that their model lifecycle processes are transparent and auditable, as well as allowing the business users to collaborate more effectively with IT, as the model moves from the analytics platform into the production, IT-led environment.

CONCLUDING REMARKS

An inability to deploy AI and machine learning at scale creates bottlenecks in analytical efforts and means that the value the models intend to generate is not realized. When a new model is trapped as a data science project, it erodes the "wow" effect of newer, more sophisticated models.

The good news is that the technologies for model deployment have also advanced in recent years, and this means that AI and machine learning can be better integrated into existing services and front-end applications, either directly or via APIs.

ENDNOTE

1. Melissa Davis, *Gartner: Accelerating AI Deployments—Paths of Least Resistance.* (Framingham, MA: IDG Connect, 2021).

CHAPTER 7

Extending the Governance Framework for Machine Learning Validation and Ongoing Monitoring

The benefits of AI and machine learning do not present themselves without risks. Internal and external stakeholders are rightly concerned about the typical challenges ranging from the ethical use of AI and machine learning to the ability to explain the workings of the algorithms, to the amplified risk of propagating bias in decision-making. However, one of the toughest challenges is creating a suitable and robust continuous performance monitoring framework that can adapt and respond to the increased model risk of AI and machine learning. Keeping up with the same number of resources and keeping costs low is a key concern for many risk managers. Having a monitoring framework in place spans beyond the regulatory and pre-production aspects of model risk management. In general, an AI and machine learning monitoring framework should be adept to handle:

- **Model degradation.** AI and machine learning tend to degrade faster than traditional and historically tuned statistical models.

- **Biased predictions.** AI and machine learning tend to identify complex and nonlinear patterns in data that are hidden from traditional models. These patterns may propagate biased decision-making or hide corrupted data. In a way, the machine learning needs to be protected from the bias in data that can contribute to unfair decisions that they are a part of. Other components of decision making are policy rules, business roles, and human-based manual overrides. All aspects that contribute to decisions, not limited to models, can result in biased predictions.

- **Balance.** High materiality models have always required a high level of human oversight. The same applies to the use of AI and machine learning: closed, fully automated, black-box systems that lack human oversight and ability to override are not recommended. There are also other key considerations to account for, such as the context in which the model will be used, and privacy implications of the data.

Typically, risk models, including those used for intra-day or near-real-time calculations, are used in settings with existing and established model governance practices in place. With the use of more advanced modeling technologies and approaches, like AI and machine learning, model risk tends to be higher (as explained in the next section), therefore near-real-time performance tracking of these models becomes critical.

A robust AI and machine learning governance framework aligns the oversight of the use of AI systems and machine learning to the corporate strategy and values of an organization. AI governance is that strategy that then defines the policies and procedures to establish accountability for the safe development, deployment, and use of AI systems and machine learning. These aspects are central tenants of Conway's law—that an organization's dysfunction always reveals itself in its products. Thus, AI and machine learning governance reflects the organization's mindset.

In 2019, the OECD defined a set of AI principles to promote the use of AI for innovation while protecting human rights.[1] Since then, regulators around the world have followed suit. In Asia, for example, the Monetary Authority of Singapore defined a model governance framework for AI systems,[2] and in Europe, the European Union is clearly differentiating between high- and low-risk AI applications with prescribed requirements for each.[3]

In addition to regulations on AI governance, in 2021, the Federal Trade Commission in the United States defined its expectations for the responsible use of AI, especially in the context of fair outcomes for consumers.[4]

In 2021, the Office of the Currency Comptroller updated its model risk management standards to take into account the use of AI and machine learning.[5] Recently, the UK government has taken one step further by publishing a set of national algorithmic transparency standards for the use of AI in the public sector.[6]

In a sense, all models are representations of reality, and by its nature, will have some degree of uncertainty and inaccuracy. The better the characteristics and the limitations of the model are understood—up front—the better informed the model validation function will be in managing and monitoring the model in production.

Specifically, in financial services, a principle-based governance framework will promote the proper use of models, the right layers of accountability and degrees of transparency, together with consistency in the development, deployment, and use of risk models.

ESTABLISHING THE RIGHT INTERNAL GOVERNANCE FRAMEWORK

Where models are used for decision-making, whether traditional or AI and machine learning, organizations should be attentive to the possible adverse consequences of decisions based on models that are incorrect or misused and should address those consequences through active model risk management. These adverse consequences may include, but are not limited potential for monetary loss, and reputational risk.

The concept of AI and machine learning governance is much debated by industry bodies. Based in part on highly publicized AI model failings (take, for example, the chatbot Tay) and misconceptions of how automated systems operate, there is a general sense of distrust in the responsible use of AI and machine learning that further highlights the need for better model governance.

Most organizations have set up strong governance frameworks for their traditional risk models. According to regulatory guidance, with the right controls in place, existing frameworks can be extended to AI and machine learning.[7]

According to the Office of the Currency Comptroller (OCC), in SR11/7, an effective model governance framework includes robust model development, implementation, and use, as well as effective validation, sound governance, policies, and controls.

The OCC highlights that model risk increases with greater model complexity, with more inputs and more uncertainty about model assumptions. With a potential broader extent of use, the potential impact, if the model goes wrong, is larger.

When it comes to effective model risk management and expectations from supervisors, organizations must prove their understanding of model inaccuracies and unintended consequences, their implications, and mitigating actions.

In general, it is helpful to align the level of governance based on the context and the materiality of the risk model. Keep in mind that the model governance approach aligns to the size of the organization and materiality of the model, as well as the impacts, if unintended consequences are realized. If additional users are using a model, then it is recommended that the model materiality be reassessed. In practice, we have found that if an organization focuses on the performance of models—be that traditional models or machine learning—at group level only, then subsidiaries can be ignored, where the materiality of the models could be vastly different. This might not create a significant exposure at the group level but could pose significant model and reputational risk at the subsidiary level.

To provide the necessary governance and oversight, for risk models that impact high-stakes risk decisions, a range of stakeholders, from external regulators to the board, to senior management, are involved in various stages of the risk model lifecycle. In addition to stakeholders directly involved in the risk model lifecycle, the right governance framework will further foster trust and transparency in the models for other users and consumers.

DEVELOPING MACHINE LEARNING MODELS WITH GOVERNANCE IN MIND

An important question to ask yourself before launching an AI or machine learning is: "How do we put the right governance guardrails in place to ensure that models from the lab put into production continue to remain fit for purpose and deliver value expected?" One approach, as mentioned, is to build stronger trust in the data, the models, and align expected outcomes with the business objectives.

Having the right people, processes, and policies in place will help standardize the treatment of AI and machine learning at the enterprise level. As many of the model development steps can be automated, AI and machine learning are often easier to develop compared to, say, traditional statistical models, but it requires higher levels of monitoring (e.g., testing of model performance once a year is not enough, as AI and machine learning needs to be monitored much more frequently, and, depending on the use case, even near-real-time).

With AI and machine learning governance, questions about model use can be raised throughout the model lifecycle:

- How were the conceptual soundness of AI and machine learning assessed?

- How were the features generated and selected?
- Can the model and its key drivers be explained in technical and nontechnical terms?
- Is the trade-off in complexity and maintenance of a more sophisticated model outweighing the use of a more interpretable benchmark model?
- How do I plan to ensure that the machine learning continues to be fit for purpose?
- How fast can the model be replaced if it shows a significant performance deterioration?

These questions and others are captured in Figure 7.1.

For these reasons, existing governance frameworks may not be sufficient to handle the increased model risk associated with AI and machine learning.

As mentioned, in general, with the use of AI and machine learning, model risk tends to be higher, as the algorithms are more sophisticated in approach and use. In addition, post-hoc explainability and interpretability add an additional layer of complexity. Keep in mind that another layer of complexity, in some AI and machine learning, stems from the use of optimized hyperparameters (explained fully in Chapter 8). There is also an increased risk of model error due to poor data quality and the risk of perpetuating societal or individual biases using biased data or biased algorithms.

Figure 7.2 captures the mentioned challenges, in addition to others, that tend to increase model risk with AI and machine learning models.

Standardized industry practices to better manage the increasing demands pertaining to model governance of AI and machine learning are still evolving with influential forces across internal and external stakeholders:

- Public pressure and advocacy to promote the ethical use of AI and machine learning.
- Compliance with laws and regulations that compel organizations to respect the rights and interests of people with respect to how they use AI and machine learning, together with personal data.

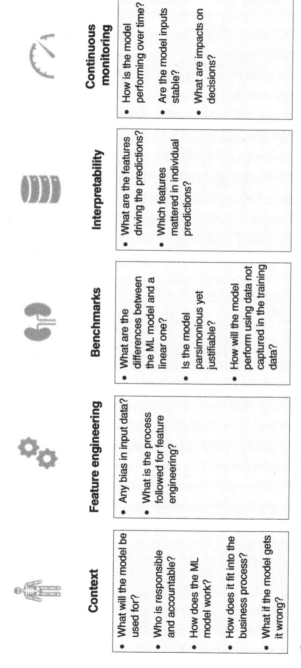

How do I explain my models to stakeholders?

Context
- What will the model be used for?
- Who is responsible and accountable?
- How does the ML model work?
- How does it fit into the business process?
- What if the model gets it wrong?

Feature engineering
- Any bias in input data?
- What is the process followed for feature engineering?

Benchmarks
- What are the differences between the ML model and a linear one?
- Is the model parsimonious yet justifiable?
- How will the model perform using data not captured in the training data?

Interpretability
- What are the features driving the predictions?
- Which features mattered in individual predictions?

Continuous monitoring
- How is the model performing over time?
- Are the model inputs stable?
- What are impacts on decisions?

Figure 7.1 Model governance questions. There are questions that the business can raise throughout the lifecycle of an AI/ML model, including during the design, development, predeployment, and monitoring phases.

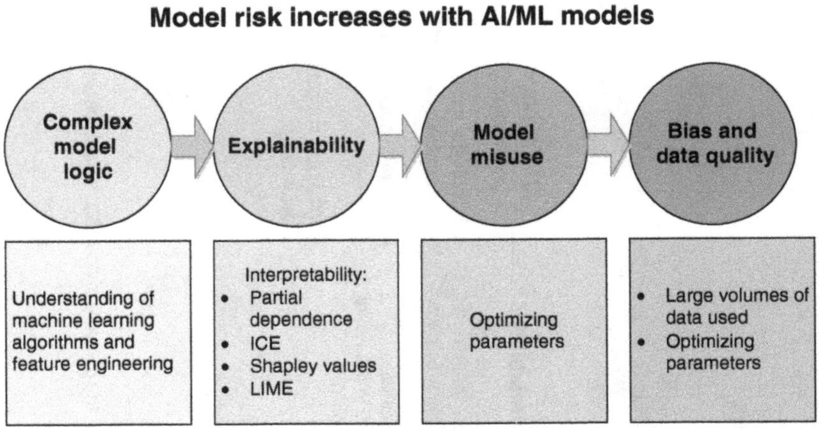

Model risk increases with AI/ML models

Figure 7.2 Model risk increases with AI/ML models. It is important to understand that the risks associated with a model tend to increase with AI/ML models, namely across the model logic, explainability, model misuse, and bias and data quality.

- Internal promotion of best practices in the development, deployment, and use of AI systems and machine learning.
- Promotion of broader explainability and transparency of AI and machine learning: purpose, design, use of the model, model architecture, key drivers, data inputs, model outputs, model limitations, and assumptions and reproducible results.
- Internal governance structures to enforce these best practices.
- Use of interpretable benchmarks.
- Independent audit of AI, machine learning, and autonomous systems.

MONITORING AI AND MACHINE LEARNING

Machine learning need governance just like other models, only more so. In part, this is because these models are designed to improve automatically through experience. Their ability to "learn" enables greater accuracy and predictability, but it can also greatly increase their model risk and result in biases based on patterns in data that they are able to identify. It is critical that organizations establish rigorous governance processes that can quickly identify when a model begins to fail, complete with defined operating controls on inputs (data) and output (model results). The dynamic nature of AI and machine learning means that it requires more frequent performance monitoring, constant data review, and benchmarking. With the increased volume of models, a better understanding of the contextual model inventory and actionable contingency plans is needed.[8]

Even when organizations have extended their model governance to AI and machine learning, there are further considerations about the ongoing monitoring of AI and machine learning that should be considered beyond those currently enacted and discussed in previous sections.

We have explained in this chapter that, traditionally, organizations have in place standard model governance frameworks that include regular monitoring reporting and reviews for regulatory and nonregulatory risk models. All risk models are typically subject to internal and external validation, which requires regular tracking of models by performance and operational computed metrics.

As new regulatory requirements necessitate the need to adjust the models and the number of risk models over time, the sophistication of modeling methods is increasing and will continue to do so with the mainstream adoption of AI and machine learning. AI and machine learning are often dynamically updated (i.e., calibrated with new data with more ease), which means that a slew of metrics will need tracking over time to ensure that the model is performing within the boundaries as expected by business goals and compliance measures.

These are best explained when taking a holistic view of the "health" of an algorithm across the dimensions listed below and shown in Figure 7.3:

- Input data and data quality.
- Features and variable importance.
- Model assumptions and limitations—made during model development, including the data limitations used to engineer features.
- Benchmarks applied and how these were derived.
- Stability at the level of the population and characteristics (or engineered features).

■ Performance of the model over time, comparing performance to benchmark.

■ Decisions made such as purely model-derived decisions or in combination with rule sets or other post-modeling processes.

Complementary to holistic model health, there are ways in which organizations can validate that the model is performing in line with expectations. These metrics can be automated and run at regular time intervals: annually, quarterly, monthly, weekly, daily, intraday, or near-real-time. A selection of metrics are included and described in

Taking a holistic view of model health

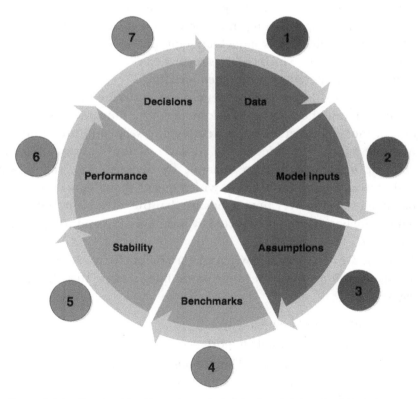

Figure 7.3 Further considerations of AI and machine learning that should be taken when taking a more holistic view of model health, including measures that can identify models that require immediate attention before drop in their performance can be measured.

more detail below: model decay, stability, robustness, interpretability, bias, and model adjustments.

Model Decay

The established industry practices for model validation typically include the monitoring of the performance of the model, the stability of model inputs, and model calibration. These metrics are all still valid for AI and machine learning. In addition, for AI and machine learning, especially models that continuously update, it is necessary to continuously monitor the models' explainability and potential for bias. Importantly, the performance monitoring results should be summarized in a way that provides understanding to users of where the root causes of issues reside, so the performance results can be reviewed in context.

For example, as mentioned, given their complexity, AI and machine learning tend to pick up relationships in the data that may be temporary. To account for temporal fluctuations, the models must be monitored more frequently.

Model degradation is typically a consequence of data or concept drift:

- *Data drift* occurs when the distributions of feature attributes change over time when compared to the model development sample. This requires monitoring of the sample data vs. production data—the complexity increases when a model is updated more frequently.
- *Concept drift* occurs when a change in market conditions or policy changes the model interpretation. In the case of a model interpretation change, typically, the development data needs to be relabeled and model retrained. Concept drift can be measured by evaluating the historical relationships between features that are driving the model's predictions.

Stability

The stability of an AI or machine learning and benchmark model is typically performed by assessing the stability of the data inputs, the population, and the features.

Population Drift

The Population Stability Index (PSI) is one way to measure that the model outcomes are stable over time. It is an established metric for traditional statistical or econometric models. It's a divergence metric that measures the distance between two distributions (e.g., the current population and the model development sample). It is often interpreted as a rule of thumb but can also be interpreted using confidence intervals, which may be more appropriate for continuous monitoring for machine learning models.[9]

Feature Drift

The population stability index can also be used to calculate divergence at the characteristic level, namely the characteristic stability index (CSI). This measures how the distributions of the model characteristic differ from the development sample.

Another approach to assess the feature stability of AI or machine learning is by bootstrapping or random perturbation. This can be done either by sub-sampling or by randomly perturbing the development data so as to create n datasets. The algorithm for selecting features is applied to n datasets, and m features are created. The stability of the features is measured by determining the similarity of the features selected across the n datasets.

It can also be calculated using the t-distributed stochastic neighbor embedding (T-SNE).

Robustness, Benchmarking, and Backtesting

The robustness of a model, whether machine learning–based or not, refers to the model's ability to generalize well on new data. Model robustness can be improved by generalization and stopping and pruning methods. Overfitting can also be evaluated by cross-validation. These tests include benchmarking, backtesting, and stability assessments.

Traditionally, benchmarking is where the results of the model are compared to a benchmark. By example, the benchmark sample could stem from the initial periods' implementation data. Backtesting is performed when the model logic is applied to historical data to evaluate how stable the predicted values are against the actual values.

Traditional models can be used as benchmarks for AI and machine learning. Benchmark models are typically developed under the same major assumptions of the AI and machine learning. The robustness and performance of both the traditional and AI or machine learning model can then be measured and compared for statistically significant differences.

Interpretability

Traditional models tend to use defined variable selection and model fitting methods that are directly explainable. For example, the parameter estimates of a generalized-linear model (GLM) can be interpreted directly, reflecting the contributions of the features, and thus the model is interpretable from its parameter estimates. The coefficients of a machine learning model like a gradient-boosting machine (GBM) cannot be interpreted directly, and so they need alternative measures of interpretability.

Variable Importance

The lack of interpretation is suboptimal for AI and machine learning, as it needs a consistent method to assess variable importance across a range of methods. A generalized way of assessing the variable importance of AI and machine learning is to fit a decision tree to approximate model predictions to identify and prioritize variables in order of importance. Another way is to create a parameter that extends the classical R2 method of linear regression that provides a description of the relationship between model predictions and input features.[10] Figure 7.4 supplies an illustrative general sample of variable importance.

Partial Dependence

Partial dependence (PD) plots are a model-agnostic explainability measure that can be used to interpret an AI and machine learning at the global level. Model-agnostic measures like PD plots are applied to supervised AI and machine learning.

Variable Name	Train Importance
curr_days_susp	81.3108
handset_age_grp	46.5221
ever_days_over_plan	30.2300
pymts_late_ltd	24.8962
billing_cycle	16.2053
avg_days_susp	15.8511
calls_care_ltd	13.3913
call_category_1	13.1900

Variable Importance

Figure 7.4 Variable importance: An example. Here, the train importance value corresponds to the contribution the variable makes to the success of the model—the higher the value, then the more plausible it is that the variable represents the true cause of prediction.

The PD plot (Figure 7.5) measures the contribution of each feature by measuring how the model prediction changes with changes in the feature values. This is done by perturbing the input data and averaging the effect of a feature for the entire data. A more detailed description of PD plots is provided in Chapter 4. Using a descriptive example, a PD plot shows the increase in prediction estimate with an increase in current payment status. The PD plot is displaying the relationship between the input feature (independent variable) and target variable. PD plots are useful to display the "marginal effect" of a variable on the prediction outcome.

Individual Conditional Expectation

Individual conditional expectation (ICE) plots (Figure 7.6) separate the PD function for each observation or at the subgroup level. They are helpful to identify trends, differences, and interactions.

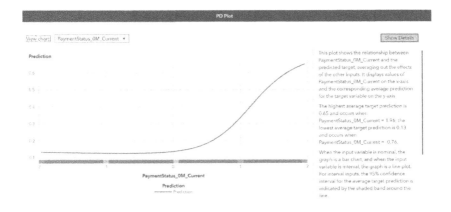

Figure 7.5 Partial dependence (PD) plot: An example. The independent variable x1 vs. the model outcome bar, after considering the average effect of other independent variables in the model.

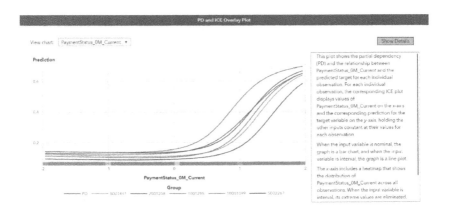

Figure 7.6 Diagrammatical representation of the individual conditional expectation (ICE) plot. The ICE plot displays the relationship to the outcome model prediction.

Shapley Values

Shapley values are another model-agnostic measure of model explainability. The Shapley value calculates the variable contributions by averaging the marginal contribution across all coalitions. This enables

Shapley values to control for variable interactions. For example, in Figure 7.7, variables rank in ascending order. The horizontal location displays whether the effect of that value is associated with a higher or lower prediction. In this example, the observation demarcated by local instance 8001441 has a predicted value of 0 in the model training data. The borrowers' current payment plan status and limit balance have contributed to the prediction.

Anomaly Detection

Ideally, anomaly detection systems for AI and machine learning should have ability to collect useful features from high-dimensional data and find deviations from normal behavior. Autoencoders can design anomaly detection systems for AI and machine learning, as they reduce the number of units in the hidden layers of a neural network, for example, to reduce the dimensionality of data. The autoencoder functions as a feature extraction method. Here, the autoencoder learns the "normal" data points—anomalies are absent from the training data. When the autoencoder reconstructs, anomalous data points will fail.[11] The failure becomes known as a *reconstruction error* and can

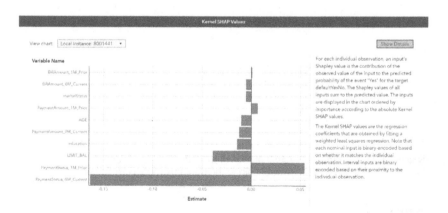

Figure 7.7 Shapley value calculation using the kernel explainer: An example.

calculate anomaly scores and label "unseen" data points after deployment of the AI and machine learning.

Bias

AI and machine learning are susceptible to either performance or results bias. We discuss the concept of performance bias in Chapter 5. Specifically, results bias refers to the model output that is statistically different for one "group" compared to another, or to benchmarks determined from the model development data or another benchmark sample. For the purposes of monitoring bias in an AI and machine learning, results bias is measured using a suitable computed metric (e.g., demographic parity), including tolerance thresholds. Bias may be introduced indirectly for various reasons, including internal policy changes, external regulatory compliance, or that there is not a sufficiently long history of observational data available for one "group" compared to another. When differences are observed, it can trigger a review to identify the cause for bias.

Model Adjustments

AI and machine learning typically utilize advanced methods to optimize the objective function of the algorithms. AI and machine learning are often regularly retrained using new training data. Risk models need retraining for several reasons. For example:

- **External conditions.** Factors such as updated interest rates, updated systems, and associated data can initiate the need to retrain models.
- **Strategy changes.** If it becomes clear during the development period that the model is not capturing business changes or changes in business strategy, the models could require retraining.
- **Business performance.** Changes in the use and performance of a model, for example, due to the COVID-19 pandemic, can trigger a model retraining effort.

COMPLIANCE CONSIDERATIONS

Regulatory bodies around the world are starting to propose regulations and compliance guidelines on all aspects of AI and machine learning, including data privacy usage, ethics guidelines, and specific model risk management frameworks. However, the depth and breadth of these regulations and compliance guidelines depends on the rate of adoption of AI and machine learning in jurisdictions. Selected compliance considerations to be aware of include:

- Global Data Protection Regulation (GDPR).
- Equal Credit Opportunity Act (ECOA)—updated CFPB for small business loans.
- SR Letter 11-7—updated guidance for AI and machine learning.
- European Commission—laying down harmonized rules on AI.
- EU guidelines for trustworthy AI.

GDPR (Global Data Protection Regulation)

This European law regulates data protection and privacy laws in the European Union and European Economic Area. Released by GDPR in 2019 was the "Ethics Guidelines for Trustworthy AI." For AI to comply with the GDPR provisions, additional factors need to be carefully considered (see Table 7.1 for a summary of key questions).

ECOA (Equal Credit Opportunity Act)

The United States Federal Trade Commission (FTC) administers a wide variety of consumer protection laws, including those that prevent unfair methods of competition in commerce and prohibit unfair and deceptive acts or practices. The FTC also has a long history of using its authority to regulate private sector uses of personal information and algorithms that directly affect consumers. One of the ways that the FTC exercises such authority is by the Equal Credit Opportunity Act (ECOA). The ECOA helps to protect consumers in gaining equal access to credit by protecting them from discrimination based

Table 7.1 Key Questions When Complying with GDPR Guidelines and AI[12]

Guideline	Explanation brief
Right to not be subject to automated decision-making	The right to not be subject to automated decision-making is prohibited only if the decision-making is based solely on automated processing and produces legal effects concerning the data subject or similarly significantly affects them. However, it is allowed if the process is done with the data subject's explicit consent, or the controller has put sufficient safeguards in place. In this scenario, the safeguards that need to be provided include: involvement of human intervention to analyze and address the system's purpose, constraints, requirements, and decisions in a clear and transparent manner, explaining the automated decision-making clearly in the privacy policy to notify clients before processing their data, and obtaining explicit consent to notify a data subject that a decision is the result of an algorithm decision and they are interacting with an AI agent like chatbot or robot or other conversational system.
Transparent processing	Data subjects should be informed of the existence and purpose of the processing, especially when the data-processing activities involve automated decision-making. Meaningful information about the logic, significance, and envisaged consequences of such processing should be explicitly transparent to users.
Right to erasure	As a result of data sharing and data openness needed to collect and collate large amounts of data for AI to be of use, it is hard for data controllers to ensure that a third-party data server implements the deleting operation or if the data required to be erased are deleted completely from other joint controllers or data processors.
Data minimization	De-identification (pseudonymization) allows more data to be used, processed, and analyzed in AI. Pseudonymization meets the GDPR principle of data minimization, unlike anonymization, which means that the data subject is no longer or not identifiable. The GDPR promotes pseudonymization as an appropriate safeguard for organizations to repurpose data without additional consent.

on protected variables such as race, color, sex, religion, age, and marital status.

In 2020 and 2021, the FTC notes that if a company uses an algorithm that either directly or indirectly through disparate impact discriminates against a protected class with respect to credit decisions, then the FTC can challenge the practice under the ECOA. In addition, the updated guidelines in 2020 and 2021 supply insights into expectations for organizations using AI. Examples include:

- **Start from the beginning.** Organizations need to find whether training datasets include disparate treatment of protected groups.
- **Testing.** Test algorithms before use and on a regular basis to make sure that they do not discriminate on the basis of abovementioned protected variables.

The fairness of algorithms can be assessed by considering these questions:

- How representative is the dataset?
- Does the data model account for biases?
- How exact are the predictions based on big data?
- Does the reliance on big data raise ethical or fairness concerns?
- Does the algorithm do more harm than good? Organizations should ask themselves if their AI and machine learning cause more harm than good. If they do, then the FTC can consider them "unfair" under section 5 of the FTC Acts and subject to enforcement measures.

SR-Letter 11-7

The Board of Governors of the Federal Reserve System and Office of the Comptroller of the Currency published the SR Letter 11-7 in 2011 titled: "Supervisory Guidance on Model Risk Management." The letter has become the gold standard for model risk management and one of the most important statements of a supervisor's expectations on management of model risk. Supervised banks and financial institutions in the United States are obligated to have implemented SR 11-7 principles into their model risk management frameworks.

Outside of the United States, a number of other supervisors have released regulatory expectations for model risk management, such as the European Central Bank (ECB), European Banking Authority (EBA), and national supervisors like the Canadian Office of the Superintendent of Financial Institutions (OSFI) and the Australian Prudential

Authority (APRA, under Prudential Standard CPS 220 Risk Management and the Credit Risk Management Prudential Standard APS 220). In particular, the ECB incorporated SR 11-7 principles into its Targeted Review of Internal Models (TRIM) in 2015.

SR 11-7 is far reaching and outlines all the regulatory expectations on risk management, including defining what a model is, and the processes and internal controls that banks must implement for all "models," irrespective of type. This helps to ensure that banks appropriately develop, implement, and use models in a controlled manner. The principles of SR 11-7 are critical, because all models, including AI and machine learning, risk sustaining losses due to inaccuracy or poor controls. The losses here can be far ranging, from inaccurate risk calculations, to costs involved with developing and implementing models, to the adverse reputational impacts of making unfair decisions.

Without a defined model risk management policy in place, the flexibility introduced by a range of model development applications can expose organizations to significant misuse and loss. In such a setting, there can also be an absence of appropriate controls and approvals, subsequent errors. Effective model risk management helps supply robustness and reduce the mentioned model risks.

EU Guidelines for Trustworthy AI

In 2021, the European Commission has legislated the use of AI systems in Europe.[13] The regulation follows a tiered, risk-based approach where AI systems are classified as high risk, in line with the intended purpose of the AI system, such as biometric identification, law enforcement, and assessing creditworthiness of natural persons. The legal requirements for high-risk AI systems pertain to data and data governance, transparency and auditability, human oversight, robustness, accuracy, and security, derived from the Ethics Guidelines of the High-Level Expert Group on Artificial Intelligence.[14]

FURTHER TAKEAWAY

Based on the risks, the wider use of AI and machine learning means that current model risk governance programs in place need to extend.

But, at the same time, it is important to understand the limitations of current model risk management programs that prevent a holistic view to model health across data, model inputs, benchmarks, stability, performance, and decisions.

It is important to note that any high-materiality model, irrespective of whether an AI and machine learning is used, either directly or indirectly, always requires a high level of human oversight. Regulatory bodies around the world are either extending their current regulation and compliance for model risk management to accommodate AI and machine learning or have created voluntary guidelines for a range of aspects of AI and machine learning, including data privacy usage and ethics.

Today, there is no global consensus on the design and deployment of ethical AI frameworks. However, within developed regulations and guidelines, the same ethical principles relating to fairness, ethics, accountability, and transparency are used. The depth and breadth of ethical AI compliance guidelines and regulations largely depend on the maturity of AI and machine learning adoption in the respective jurisdictions. For example, regulators in Asia Pacific are continuing to address ethical AI frameworks to help ensure that fairness objectives are achieved (e.g., the Australian government recently released the "AI ethics framework," and the Hong Kong Monetary Authority has released regulatory guidance in the form of the "RegTech Adoption Practice Guide" that includes prerequisites for an "AI governance framework")

CONCLUDING REMARKS

With the use of AI and machine learning, risk departments should broaden their thinking to extend their performance monitoring framework so that transparency of AI and machine learning can be achieved without overly depending on manual code. By dynamically tracking a range of interconnected categories—including, but not limited to, the input data, model decay, and model robustness, risk departments can better understand potential AI and machine learning limitations and proactively identify issues that may lead to model failure. Regulatory bodies and central banks also expect risk departments to adhere to certain compliance measures when validating AI and machine learning. We have explained the main concepts in this chapter.

However, even in the absence of clearly defined regulatory expectations of model risk management as outlined in SR 11-7, model risk management should still be top of mind, as the model risks associated with AI and machine learning can cause quantifiable loss, from inaccurate risk calculations, to the costs involved with developing and implementing models, to adverse impacts of making unfair decisions. These risks are worsened when AI and machine learning function outside of a robust model risk management framework that governs the development, deployment, and use of the models.

ENDNOTES

1. Artificial intelligence, https://www.oecd.org/going-digital/ai/principles/

2. Personal Data Protection Commission, *Model Artificial Intelligence Governance Framework, 2ⁿᵈ ed.* (Singapore: SG:D, Infocomm Media Development Authority, and Personal Data Protection Commission, 2020), https://www.pdpc.gov.sg/-/media/files/pdpc/pdf-files/resource-for-organisation/ai/sgmodelaigovframework2.pdf

3. European Commission, *Proposal for a Regulation of the European Parliament and of the Council: Laying Down Harmonised Rules on Artificial Intelligence (Artificial Intelligence Act) and Amending Certain Union Legislative Acts*, Eur-Lex, Brussels, (April 21, 2021), https://eur-lex.europa.eu/legal-content/EN/TXT/?qid=1623335154975&uri=CELEX%3A52021PC0206

4. Elisa Jillson, *Aiming for truth, fairness, and equity in your company's use of AI*, Federal Trade Commission (April 19, 2021), https://www.ftc.gov/news-events/blogs/business-blog/2021/04/aiming-truth-fairness-equity-your-companys-use-ai

5. Office of the Comptroller of the Currency, *Safety and Soundness, Model Risk Management*, Version 1.0 (August 2021), https://www.occ.treas.gov/publications-and-resources/publications/comptrollers-handbook/files/model-risk-management/pub-ch-model-risk.pdf

6. Government of the United Kingdom, *Algorithmic Transparency Standard* (2021), https://www.gov.uk/government/collections/algorithmic-transparency-standard#:~:text=The%20Algorithmic%20Transparency%20Standard%20is,making%20in%20the%20public%20sector

7. Patrice Alexander Ficklin, Tom Pahl, and Paul Watkins, *Innovation Spotlight: Providing Adverse Action Notices When Using AI/ML Models* (Washington, DC: Consumer Financial Protection Bureau, 2020).

8. David Asermely, *Whitepaper: Machine Learning Model Governance* (Cary, NC: SAS Institute Inc., 2021).

9. Bilal Yurdakul, *Statistical Properties of Population Stability Index*, PhD, dissertation (Western Michigan University, ScholarWorks, April 2018), https://scholarworks.wmich.edu/dissertations/3208/

10. Brian D. Williamson, Peter B. Gilbert, Marco Carone, and Noah Simon, "Nonparametric variable importance assessment using machine learning techniques," *Biometrics* 77 (1) (March 2021): 9–22.

11. Sabtain Ahmad, Kevin Stype-Rekowski, Sasho Nedelkoski, and Odej Kao, *Autoencoder-based Condition Monitoring and Anomaly Detection Method for Rotating Machines* (Cornell University, Arvix, 2021).

12. Andrea Tang, "Making AI GDPR compliant," *ISACA Journal* (5) (2019), https://www.isaca.org/resources/isaca-journal/issues/2019/volume-5/making-ai-gdpr-compliant

13. European Commission, *Proposal for a Regulation of the European Parliament.*

14. European Commission, *Ethics guidelines for trustworthy AI* (April 8, 2019), https://digital-strategy.ec.europa.eu/en/library/ethics-guidelines-trustworthy-ai

CHAPTER 8

Optimizing Parameters for Machine Learning Models and Decisions in Production

We can define optimization as the act, process, or method that is employed to find the "best" element from a set of alternatives based on the objectives, such as maximizing yield, while satisfying all the constraints. Within the context of a current business problem, this "best" element can be far-reaching: from a system, decision, or technical design. "Problems" can include but are not limited to:

- Capital allocation across portfolios to maximize yield
- Efficient use of resources to minimize waste
- Optimal decision path generation with the least amount of information

For example, to optimize capital across portfolios, the allocation of credit risk mitigants to credit risk exposures under different regulatory regimes can be done with a specific objective in mind. Here, the allocation is optimized in a way that allows a firm to reduce their regulatory capital requirements within the context of a regulatory framework. Here, the regulatory requirements are the constraints within the optimization problem.

In mathematical terms, optimization refers to the act of minimizing or maximizing a value function subjected to constraints as an expression. The function and constraints can be linear or nonlinear. Mathematical optimization is integral and extensively used in AI and machine learning (e.g., minimizing a "loss function" subject to constraints). This is achieved by applying an optimization routine to improve the accuracy of the algorithm based on the provided training data by reducing the error in predictions.[1]

Mathematicians have developed optimization algorithms for many decades. For the modern-day risk practitioner, selecting the best algorithm and specification can be a daunting task. The choice of algorithm impacts the processing time, efficiency, and accuracy of the outcome. But before we describe the use of optimization for machine learning, it is best to describe what is meant by *optimizing a value function that is subject to constraints* as mentioned earlier.

Taking a practical risk management example, a commercial bank may want to minimize the variance of returns (the objective function) while keeping their loss rates within risk appetite over t years (the constraints) and optimize the AI or machine learning accordingly.

OPTIMIZATION FOR MACHINE LEARNING

Even though the range of optimization applications in AI and machine learning is wide, two main optimization problems depend on whether the loss function is convex or nonconvex.[2]

Convex optimization has only one "best" solution, as the assumption is that a single local optimum exists—that is also the global optimum. Such a minimum exists that is determinable using a variety of well-tested and validated methods. Thus, the search area for convex optimization (Figure 8.1) in itself takes on a convex shape, whereby following the negative gradient a local minimum is reached.

Nonconvex optimization has multiple locally optimal solutions for the problem. Historically, most optimization problems in a machine learning context were considered convex; however, in recent years, with the application of neural networks and deep learning, the use of nonconvex optimization methods has grown. These algorithms work in the nonconvex landscape (Figure 8.2) (i.e., where there is more than one local minimum and the optimization of these is to efficiently find the local minima, because in this case a global minimum is impossible to prove).

Of course, there are also times when the objective function is concave. These are simply the negative of a convex function where the same principles apply.

When optimizing machine learning, the machine learning fit function is approximated by optimizing the parameters so that the

Convex f = x*x + y*y

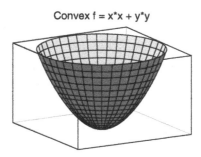

Figure 8.1 Convex optimization. The search area for a convex optimization takes on a convex shape where the objective function finds a local minima that is itself a global minimum.

Nonconvex f = x*y +0.3*y*y

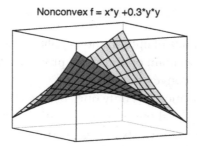

Figure 8.2 Nonconvex optimization. The search area for a nonconvex optimization has more than one local minima.

objective function is either minimized or maximized. To do that, there may be times when the input variables are restricted. These restrictions are constraints. Constraints define the feasible space over which the objective function is optimized. If the constraint requires a constant change applied to each variable, then the constraint is an *equality constraint* that decomposes to a *linear constraint*. Conversely, if the constraint is unequal for variables and can be achieved unilaterally, then the constraint is an *inequality constraint*. When applying these concepts together for machine learning optimization we get the following:

- A problem is convex if the objective is convex, equality constraints are linear if present, and all inequality constraints are concave.
- A problem is nonconvex if it is not convex. At least one is true: the objective is nonconvex, nonlinear equality constraints are present, or at least one nonlinear inequality constraint is not concave.

Of course, there are myriad ways to solve convex or nonconvex optimization problems. This is because the choice of algorithm to use as the solver depends on the application as well as the analytical method. The intention of the section is not to explain all algorithms available as solvers for convex and nonconvex optimization. By way of an introduction, we'll focus on machine learning function optimization that involves the use of solvers, the values of hyperparameters, as well as model fit optimization using stochastic gradient descent. Here are three types of solvers:

1. **Large-scale nonlinear constrained solvers.** Interior-point and active-set algorithms are good examples. These tend to be applied to business models that have nontrivial constraints.

2. **Large-scale unconstrained solvers.** Examples include the nonlinear conjugate gradient (CG), limited-memory Broyden-Fletcher-Goldfarb-Shanno (LBFGS), stochastic gradient decent (SGD), and the Adam algorithm. These tend to be applied to machine learning optimization problems where a single loss function is minimized.

3. **Derivative-free optimization solvers.** These tend to be very effective at smaller dimensional problems as they require little structure to the objective and constraints to operate. They are often the best fit for tuning hyperparameters.

Hyperparameters broadly fall into two categories: model training parameters that relate to the model architecture (e.g., the number of layers of a neural network and neurons in each layer) and solver parameters such as the learning rate or momentum of an algorithm. The choice of solver and the solver settings will significantly affect the training process.

In the next sections, we will discuss each of the solvers in more detail.

MACHINE LEARNING FUNCTION OPTIMIZATION USING SOLVERS

As defined earlier, there are many solvers to optimize an objective function, and these are dependent on whether the function to solve is convex or nonconvex. In the next section, we detail selected examples of solvers based on whether the objective function is convex or nonconvex.

Solvers for When the Target Objective Function Is Convex

When the objective function is convex, a solver needs to find one global minimum. Some solvers satisfy constraints while optimizing the objective function. Typically, solvers perform this by utilizing either an interior-point method or an active-set method. Interior-point methods start in the interior of the feasible region and use barrier functions to impose constraints. Active-set methods look to find a solution by quickly guessing the set of active constraints.

If the active constraints are known, then inactive constraints may be discarded and a much simpler solution can be efficiently reached. For this reason, despite the run-time of the algorithm being higher (referred to as "worst-case complexity"), active-set methods can outperform their interior-point counterpart. They are often the method of choice when only variable bounds are present (e.g., there are no other general constraints). The method stops when a workable point is found within the feasible region; at such a point, any attempt to further improve the objective will violate at least one constraint. The weights that achieve these balance points are known as *dual variables*; that is, they are multipliers of the constraint gradients such that the objective gradients equal the scaled sum of the constraint gradients. A Lagrangian function is often used to describe this system mathematically and hence dual variables are often called *Lagrange multipliers*.

Solvers for the Target Objective Function That Is Nonconvex

When the problem is nonconvex, there are two options to try:

1. If the problem is large scale, a multistart option can be used, which essentially applies local solvers at a diverse set of (often randomly generated) points and then returns the best. A multistart method tends work best at higher dimensions.

2. In lower dimensions, where derivative-free methods are used, deployment of sophisticated sampling methods can be performed that conduct global and local searches simultaneously. Because these do not require gradients to perform optimization, they are more generally applied, although convergence to even a local solution is not in all cases guaranteed. Because they make little assumptions on the problem itself, they are often referred to as black-box solvers.[3] Note that black-box solvers do not require the nonlinear problem, and its associated aim

and constraints, to be continuous or smooth. The algorithms deployed by the black-box solver utilize genetic algorithms or the generating set search algorithm, and these are described in more detail below:[4]

- Genetic algorithms are a family of local search algorithms that search for best solutions by applying principles of natural selection and evolution. Here, *first a sample population of random candidates gets selected,* and the target objective function evaluated for each member of the first population. Individual members of the iteration that are current are stochastically chosen, and only the members with the best objective values as solutions are chosen. Therefore, they are considered more "fit" than others, and are thus selected for the next iteration. There are times when solutions can pass onto a crossover operator or a mutation operator as part of the next iteration. The search space is defined by variable ranges, and the crossover operation allows the search to move to new areas of the search space (best characteristics of "parent" solutions are combined to create "offspring"—the combination is a new area of the search space).

  Mutation operators randomly vary the solution, so that the search over the solution space performs in a way that prevents the convergence at the local minimum to be premature.

- Generating set search algorithms that search for improved points along a positive-spanning set of the search direction. In two dimensions, this could be north, east, south, west, for example. A positive-spanning set is needed to prove convergence to local optimal points when certain assumptions implicitly hold (such as continuity and smoothness). Such conditions are not needed, however, for the algorithm to be applied. Because they are using a minimal set of samples per iteration compared to a genetic algorithm, they are much better at quickly finding a local solution. Thus, using the genetic algorithm as a global search algorithm paired with a generating set search algorithm to refine the promising points found by the genetic algorithm can lead to a robust and efficient hybrid solver.

TUNING OF PARAMETERS

There are two broad classes of parameters that require tuning during AI and machine learning model development. These can be optimized during model training or external to the model training process. There are typically hyperparameters associated with model-training (e.g., number of layers in a neural network and the number of neurons at each layer) and the solvers used for training (e.g., learning rate, momentum).

Settings for both the model training parameters and solver parameters of hyperparameters can significantly influence the accuracy of the models. Table 8.1 lists examples of parameter entities and hyperparameter attributes across both model training parameters and solver parameters for a selection of algorithms.

Table 8.1 Key Algorithms and Their Associated Parameter Entities, Including Model Training Parameters and Solver Parameters of Hyperparameters.

Algorithm	Parameter entities	Hyperparameters attributes
Linear regression	▪ Coefficients of the linear regression equation include the intercept term (constant) and betas (coefficients for the independent variables). ▪ The main estimation methods for the coefficients are ordinary least squares (OLS), simple averaging method (SAM), and stochastic gradient descent (using both the learning rate and epochs) to estimate parameters.	The stepwise regression approach to use can consist of Backward, Elasticent, Forward, Forwardswap, LAR, LASSO, None or Stepwise methods, and what cut-off values for adding/removing terms, such as the significance level for entry when the significance level is used as the select or stop criterion, and the significance level for removal when the significance level is used as the select or stop criterion.
Logistic regression	Coefficients of the logistic regression equation include the intercept term (constant) and the betas (coefficients for the independent variables). The main estimation methods are maximum likelihood or stochastic gradient descent (using both the learning rate and epochs) to estimate the logistic regression algorithm parameters.	Hyperparameters include, for example, the model selection method and use that can consist of Backward, Forward, LASSO, None, or Stepwise methods, the significance levels for entry/removal, and the lassobase regularization parameter for the LASSO methods and the number of steps for the LASSO method.

Algorithm	Parameter entities	Hyperparameters attributes
Quantile regression	Each quantile level, the distinct set of regression coefficients include the intercept and betas (coefficients for the independent variables).	None
General linear model	For the transformed response in terms of the link function and the independent variables, the coefficients are based on a linear relationship: the intercept term (constant) and the betas (coefficients for the independent variables). Maximum likelihood estimation (MLE) rather than ordinary least squares (OLS) estimates the parameters. MLE relies on large-sample approximations.	The stepwise regression approach to use that can consist of Backward, Elasticent, Forward, Forwardswap, LAR, LASSO, None or Stepwise methods, and what cut-off values for adding/removing terms such as the significance level for entry when the significance level is used as the select or stop criterion, and the significance level for removal when the significance level is used as the select or stop criterion.
Decision trees	The parameters of decision trees such as classification and regression trees (CART) are those that change the tree structure from the inside. Recursive partitioning parameters that define the tree splits are internal to the algorithm and thus determine how the tree grows, such as cost complexity and reduced error methods.	▦ Maximum depth ▦ Minimum leaf size ▦ Interval input bins ▦ Grow criterion
Random forests	Parameters include those on how the trees are split internally using the class/interval target criterion to apply, maximum number of branches, and how missing values as attributes are used.	▦ Maximum depth ▦ Minimum leaf size ▦ Number of interval bins ▦ Number of trees ▦ In-bag sample proportion ▦ Number of inputs per split
Gradient boosting machines	Parameters are either tree-specific, boosting, or miscellaneous. ▦ Tree-specific parameters: the minimum number of samples needed for splitting events, the minimum number of samples needed in a terminal leaf, the fraction of the total number of samples needed in a terminal leaf (weight-based), and the maximum number of leaves.	▦ L1 regularization ▦ L2 regularization ▦ Learning rate ▦ Maximum depth ▦ Minimum leaf size ▦ Number of interval bins ▦ Number of inputs per split ▦ Number of trees ▦ Subsample rate

(Continued)

Table 8.1 (Continued)

Algorithm	Parameter entities	Hyperparameters attributes
	▪ Boosting parameter is the number of sequential trees for modeling. ▪ Miscellaneous parameters: the loss function used to minimize each split, initialization of the output that is needed when the outcome of another model is used as the initial estimates for a GBM (gradient boosting machine), the random sample number used for seeding to allow for this number to be fixed but this fixing still allows for random samples to be seeded, verbose that allows for different values to be generated as outputs when the model fits, warm start that allows for additional trees to be fitted on previous fits of a model, and presort that automatically selects the data to be presorted to reduce split time.	
Neural networks	▪ Parameters include the activation function, which is a mathematical transformation like tanh(x). Bias that is like the intercept in a linear model, and weights of the connections between neurons either in the hidden layers or the output layer. ▪ Other parameters vary depending on the type of activation function used—e.g., the slope parameter for negative values of the nonlinear parametric ReLu activation function.	▪ Number of hidden layers ▪ Number of neurons in each hidden layer ▪ L1 weight decay ▪ L2 weight decay ▪ Learning rate ▪ Annealing rate

Algorithm	Parameter entities	Hyperparameters attributes
Support vector machines	The three classes of parameters are: ▪ Regularization that decides how much to penalize based on the misclassification points ▪ Those included in the kernel function, such as the kernel types (linear, radial basis function, polynomial or sigmoid) and the kernel coefficient for each of the kernel functions ▪ The £-insensitivity value that defines a margin of tolerance with no penalty to errors	▪ Penalty ▪ Polynomial degree
Bayesian network	The parameters are dependent on the complexity of the network. This complexity is based on the probability distribution over the n variables—that is, the probability of every combination state that represents the relationship between the variables. The parameters are: ▪ Prescreen predictors—specifies whether to prescreen variables using independence tests between the target and each input variable. ▪ Use variable selection—specifies whether to select variables using conditional independence tests between the target and each input variable based on the network. ▪ Independence test statistic—the statistic used for the independence test significance level that specifies the significance level (p-value) for independence testing using the values from the independence test significance level.	▪ Network structure ▪ Maximum parents ▪ Parenting method ▪ Number of bins

Tuning hyperparameter values is a critical aspect of the model training process. The approach to finding the ideal values for hyperparameters (tuning a model to a particular dataset) has been a manual effort and thus time consuming. For guidance in setting these values, risk modelers often rely on their experience using machine learning. However, even with expertise in machine learning and their hyperparameters, the best settings of these hyperparameters will change significantly with different data; it is often difficult to prescribe the hyperparameter values based on previous experience. The ability to explore alternative configurations in a more guided and automated manner helps reduce the need for manual effort. Below are common approaches used for automated hyperparameter tuning:

- **Grid search.** Each hyperparameter of interest is discretized into a desired set of values. Models are trained and assessed for all combinations of the values across all values for the hyperparameters (as a grid). The values of the hyperparameters are the levels of the grid. The combinations of potential values of the hyperparameters that are searched across each "grid" depend on the levels of the hyperparameters. For example, for each "grid" where all parameters have the same number of levels, the search number of total combinations is calculated using n (levels) raised to the power of k (parameters). The processing for grid search quickly becomes prohibitively expensive. An example to illustrate how expensive this grows is with GBM from Table 8.1.

  For the 9 hyperparameters and assuming the same number of levels (say 3), the grid can end up with 19,683 combinations.

- **Random search.** Candidate models are trained and assessed by using random combinations of hyperparameter values. In random search, distributions for the hyperparameters are defined, either uniformly or with a sampling method. Random search runs faster than an exhaustive grid search because a random sample of combinations is selected. It is important to note that with random search, no learning from previously tried hyperparameter values or combinations of values takes place. This means that there is an element of "luck" that takes place for the selection of the individual hyperparameter values and their combinations.

- **Latin hypercube sampling.** This method follows an experimental design in which samples are exactly uniform across each hyperparameter but random in combinations. The approach is more structured than a pure random search and allows for a more uniform sample of each hyperparameter, which can help identify hyperparameter importance even if the best combination is not discovered.

- **Optimization.** Here, the search is based on an objective of minimizing the model validation error, so each "evaluation" from the algorithm's perspective is a full cycle of model training and validation. These methods are designed to make use of fewer evaluations and thus save on computation time. It is important to note that with optimization for hyperparameter search, "learning" occurs. The learning occurs with previously tried configurations that influence the selection of new configurations while minimizing the loss function. The trade-off is that fewer configurations can be evaluated in parallel. Theoretically, with enough machines, grid or random configurations could be evaluated in parallel, but with optimization the parallelization is limited, as iterations are necessary to learn.

- **Local search optimization.** Like "derivative-free optimization," this refers to a class of tuning algorithms where many different individual algorithms can be applied independently. A specific implementation of local search optimization that is not a standard approach is the hybrid framework for a distributed environment that can help overcome the challenges and expense of hyperparameter optimization.

OTHER OPTIMIZATION ALGORITHMS FOR RISK MODELS

Optimization algorithms exist for specific machine learning models, including those for logistic regression and neural networks. In this section, we list each of these algorithms.

Logistic Regression

Each of the following techniques are for nonlinear optimization that can be encountered with logistic regression algorithms where repeated computation is needed for the optimization criterion, the gradient vector (first-order partial derivative), and some of the Hessian matrix (second-order partial derivatives).

- Conjugate-gradient
- Double dogleg
- Dual quasi-Newton
- Nelder-Mead simplex
- Newton-Raphson
- Newton-Raphson with ridging
- Trust-region

Neural Networks

- **Stochastic gradient decent.** The optimization problem of this algorithm is to solve for the weights. This algorithm is a variation of gradient descent in which, instead of calculating the gradient of the loss over all observations to update the weights at each step, a "mini-batch" random sample of observations is used to estimate loss. The sampling occurs without replacement until all observations have been used. The performance of stochastic gradient descent, as with all optimization algorithms, depends on control parameters for which no default values are applicable to all problems. Stochastic gradient descent parameters include control parameters such as:
  - A learning rate that controls the step size for selecting new weights
  - An adaptive decay rate and an annealing rate to adjust the learning rate for each weight and time
  - A momentum parameter to avoid slow oscillations
  - A size for sampling a subset of observations

MACHINE LEARNING MODELS AS OPTIMIZATION TOOLS

We have discussed mathematical optimization and how that is used in algorithms. However, and as explained at the beginning of the chapter, optimization refers to an act, process, or method that is employed to make "something" as fully functional or effective as possible based on a current problem. That "something" can be far reaching in risk management—from a system, decision, a technical design, and of course the machine learning algorithms. What follows are examples of the business applications in risk management that require optimization to maximize effectiveness.

Decision Science Optimization Tool to Reduce Credit Decisioning Policy Rules

Although the policy rules that are applied to consumer loan applications represent a latent loss function of the individual credit risk profile, they also reflect the risk appetite of an organization. This means that the policy rules expand and contract to tighten or loosen credit policy over time. They are also needed to either contribute or act as reason code generators to approve or decline loans. However, policy rules are often applied subjectively, which often slows down decision response time.

Furthermore, although policy rules are critical for lending decisions, there are five overlooked aspects of policy rules that create opportunities for optimization:

1. **Univariate.** Policy rules are typically applied as univariate rules (IF, AND, OR, WHERE), and require continuous updates for regulatory and other compliance reasons.

2. **Repetitive.** To keep up with regulations and compliance, often the rules increase in number due to the creation of new rules. This creates a doubling-up effect across policy categories and leads to unnecessary complexity.

3. **Slow decisions.** A plethora of policy rules result in slow decision response times and a lack of clarity on which individual policies or combinations of policies contribute to a decision.

4. **Rationalization.** Risk teams may optimize the number of rules by simply ascertaining the frequency of records captured by them (considering the hit rate). Rules with a low hit rate, on average over a specified time, may be removed manually.

5. **Regulatory pressure.** Increased demand due to laws governing conduct aspects, and other regulatory mandates means that any effort to reduce policy rules using hit rates are ineffective.

A decision science optimization tool that uses approximation (or function approximate) machine learning to simulate what the final decision will be could:

- Enhance optimization of policy rules
- Replace rules or combinations of rules
- Anticipate rules required to make the final decisions
- Better the customer experience by reducing decision time

The decision science optimization tool carefully considers the lending process flow of a retail loan application. Policy rules are often implemented into a decision engine, but some banks run credit models (i.e., scorecards) against applications first and then policy rules to ensure that credit declines are not overridden by policy rules.

Irrespective of the sequence of running a policy rule or credit model on the loan application, decisions made are often a blend of models and policy rules, and these can be adjusted by manual assessors. Manual assessors can override automated decisions. In some cases, the override process prolongs the time to decision and can result in non-take-up of approved applications. Excessive amounts of policy overrides are often associated with too many policy rules and complexity.

The design principles shown in Figure 8.3 are explained below:

- Typically, an initial scorecard assesses the credit risk of the application.

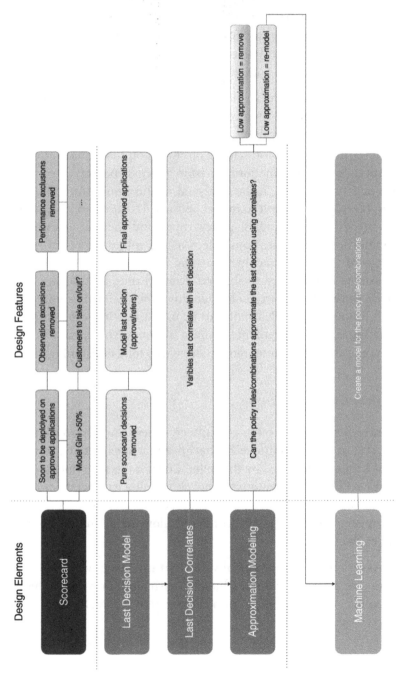

Figure 8.3 The design principles of a decision science optimization tool to reduce policy rules. Importantly, the tool should allow for both forces of the decisioning to be assessed —these being both the scorecard and policy rules.

- For policy rule optimization, a two-step process is performed:
  - First, identify the variables that correlate with the last decision.
  - Then, use these to determine how well the categories of policy rules can be approximated.

- Policy rule categories with low approximation can either be removed or, if still required, the sub-segments can be modeled using machine learning.

Importantly, the decision science optimization tool could allow for both aspects of the originations decision process, namely the credit models and policy rules, to be analyzed at the same time. The last decision is typically difficult to model because decisions on loan applications are driven by models, policy rules, and manual assessment interventions, and thus are both objective and subjective in nature.

The tool provides machine learning insights, but importantly, these insights can be used to shorten decision time by utilizing final approvals or rejections early in the lending process. Furthermore, the strength of the machine learning can be used to optimize revenue by determining customer segments that are high net worth, have ability to repay, and should not undergo unnecessarily long decisioning times.

Collateral Optimization

Collateral refers to assets, other guarantees, or securities that a counterparty agrees to transfer to the seller that are equal or exceed the receivables and liabilities provided by the seller. Collateral acts to mitigate the risk to the seller of the counterparty not completing its agreement if, for example, the counterparty defaults.[5] Thus, collateral is the asset that the buyer transfers to the seller as securities.[6] Below are definitions to help further explain the terms:

- **Assets** refer to anything of value that can be converted to cash in the future. Examples include cash and cash equivalents, bonds, equity, money market instruments, real estate, and cryptocurrencies.

▧ **Counterparties** are individuals or legal entities, like a business, commercial bank, or government body.

Managing collateral requires multiple decisions that involve complexity, because the management depends on whether the bank is acting as the seller or counterparty (as is the case in the capital markets). At a general level, these decisions include the following:

▧ The type of security.

▧ Value to assign to the underlying asset of the collateral.

▧ Opportunity costs of the collateral—these relate to the underlying asset administration costs, and the counterparty risk.

When there are only a few available assets to be distributed between a handful of exposures, the management of the collateral is quite simple and intuitive, meaning that the management of the collateral can easily be done manually.[7] When the available assets, exposures, and counterparties grow beyond a few, it is faster to optimize collateral allocation using algorithmic approaches including machine learning. Here, the optimization exercise is to solve which allocation of collateral results in the lowest cost to the bank, but one that meets the agreements made between the seller and the counterparty and margin call requirements of the assets.[8] As an example, the objective functions of a set of models are listed below:

▧ **Cost model.** This model minimizes collateral cost as well as funding costs.

▧ **Allocation model.** This can be done by for example, ranking the assets from lowest to highest by the cost model, or by linear programming.[9]

CONCLUDING REMARKS

The use of AI, machine learning, and advanced analytics for optimization is a rapidly evolving field. In this chapter, machine learning algorithmic optimization was explained. These involve the use of solvers, the automated tuning of hyperparameters, and model training optimization using stochastic gradient descent. In addition, optimization algorithms with embedded machine learning are powerful tools to solve risk-specific business problems. Keep in mind that although powerful, optimization is mathematically complex and may involve intensive compute resources. The good news is that there are automated ways to apply optimization using machine learning that transfer some of the complexity to help streamline decision-making, so that risk departments can focus on the business value that optimization can generate.

ENDNOTES

1. Stephen Boyd, and Lieven Vandenberghe, *Convex Optimization*, 1st ed. (Stanford, CA: Cambridge University Press, 2004).
2. Boyd and Vandenberghe, *Convex Optimization*.
3. Ed Hughes, Steve Gardner, Josh Griffin, and Oleg Golovidov, *The New solve-Blackbox Action in SAS® Optimization 8.5* (SAS Global Forum, 2020). Paper SAS4494-2020. https://www.sas.com/content/dam/SAS/support/en/sas-global-forum-proceedings/2020/4494-2020.pdf
4. SAS Institute Inc., *SAS® Optimization 8.3: Mathematical Optimization Procedures* (Cary, NC: SAS Institute Inc., 2018).
5. Adriano A. Rampini and S. Viswanathan, "Collateral, risk management, and the distribution." *Journal of Finance* 65(6) (2010): 2293–2322.
6. Manmohan. Singh, *The Changing Collateral Space* (Washington, D.C, USA: International Monetary Fund (IMF), 2013).
7. Akber Datoo, "Collateral – Enforceability, Reform and Optimisation." In: NA, ed. *Legal Data for Banking: Business Optimisation and Regulatory Compliance* (Hoboken, NJ: John Wiley & Sons, 2019), 115–154.
8. Ami Arbel, *Exploring Interior-point Linear Programming: Algorithms and Software* (Cambridge, MA: Foundations of computing. MIT Press, 1993).
9. Alexander Schrijver, *Theory of Linear and Integer Programming*. 1st ed. (Hoboken, NJ: John Wiley & Sons, 1998).

CHAPTER 9

The Interconnection between Climate and Financial Stability

Over decades, the discussions about climate change have been topics of both wide debate and scientific research. Questions have ranged from *"What is climate change?"* to *"How can climate change be any different from natural climate variations?"* to *"Are we heading to a climate apocalypse?"* The accumulated scientific research found that globally, atmospheric temperatures are rising above natural variations with potentially devastating consequences to people, communities, and impacting financial stability.

The tragedy of the horizon, as Mark Carney put it in his groundbreaking speech in 2015,[1] is also a tragedy of inequality where countries who are the bigger greenhouse gas emitters are also likely more resilient to the physical and transition risks of climate change.

Many industries have taken steps to better understand, quantify, and report on climate-related risks, and to devise strategies to mitigate the impacts of climate change. It is important to note that these initiatives are in their infancy. In the financial services industry, central banks, and regulators are raising awareness about the financial risks and opportunities of climate change. Recently, in 2021, more than 450 financial institutions representing $130 trillion of total assets committed to net-zero targets by 2050, as part of the Glasgow Financial Alliance for Net Zero (GFANZ).

It highlighted that the financial services industry has a key role to play in tackling climate change, in:

- Ensuring the stability and resilience of the financial system in facing emerging risks.

- Helping to manage the financial and nonfinancial risks associated with climate change.

- Helping to lead the transition through portfolio decarbonization and greening initiatives and supporting the transition toward a more sustainable economy through lending and investment activities, including the creation of the Network for Greening the Financial System (NGFs) by a group of Central Banks and supervisors in 2017.[2]

Many central banks, regulators, and industry bodies have published guidelines and policies to address financial risks posed by climate change. While we do observe convergence in some areas of guidance across jurisdictions—for example, the use of forward-looking scenario analysis and standardized reporting—for the Board and the risk management function, a profusion of divergent regulatory frameworks, guidance, and standards exist. What is becoming clearer is that financial institutions are focusing on a broad range of topics covering climate-related calculations, controls, conduct, communication, culture, and their customers. These considerations include:

- Development of plausible, short- and long-term climate risk narratives in the form of forward-looking scenarios that involve warming potential, supported by climate models that incorporate physical and transition risks.

- Identification of the impacts on financial risks such as credit and market risks and disclosures that involve forward-looking models, insights, and metrics.

- Standardized reporting and calculations that will ensure a level playing field and comparable results.

- Appropriate levels of conduct to ensure artificial "greening" of portfolios does not occur, referred to as *greenwashing*.

- Adherence to national laws. Regular communication with regulators, investors, employees, clients, and the public.

- Development of internal environmental risk assessment capacity.

- Engagement with stakeholders, especially those expected to be impacted by climate change.

- Support and engagement with customers during the responsible transition period that the institution decides to take.

As we find ourselves in the decisive decade in transitioning to a lower carbon economy, there is an urgency for financial institutions to help manage both the financial and nonfinancial risks. In the next section, we will be discussing more details.

MAGNITUDE OF CLIMATE INSTABILITY: UNDERSTANDING THE "WHY" OF CLIMATE CHANGE RISK MANAGEMENT

Firstly, it is important to understand the main issues, the science, and the data before discussing possible solutions. In the financial services industry, as in other industries, climate risk is becoming mainstream in corporate decision-making: the magnitude of climate instability will impact most aspects of financial decision-making. To assess and address climate change, a *scientific* approach can be borrowed—where a *scientific* mindset is used to investigate historic data and observational studies, build questions, and then formulate a hypothesis. However, this approach has its own limitations, as there is no historical precedent for climate change.

Climate Change Crisis: Not Just about CO_2 Emissions

Discussions on climate change, and whether it is indeed an emergency or real, are not new and have been around for decades. However, at the time of writing, 97% of climate scientists agree that climate change exists.[3] Research on the impacts of climate change shifted to forward-looking scenarios based on projected emissions grouped as greenhouse gases. Greenhouse gas emissions are a byproduct of both the extraction and burning of fossil fuels. It has an impact on the climate, that is, increasing the atmospheric temperature, but it also impacts human health.[4]

More specifically, polluting facilities that process and distribute fossil fuels increase the levels of greenhouse gases in the atmosphere, leading to a warming effect. The main culprits are CO_2 and other pollutants such as methane, but also include nitrous oxide and fluorinated gases.[5] These facilities create 80% of CO_2 and 30% of methane pollution.[6] Accumulated evidence has suggested that other contributors to climate change are human activities such as natural gas drilling, transportation, farming, deforestation, and fertilizers.[7]

Research indicates that human activities contribute to the association between greenhouse gas emissions and the average rise in the planet's temperature observed in the last century.[8] More dramatically, in recent years, since 1975, the planet's temperature has risen by 2.3 to 2.7 degrees Fahrenheit or 1.5 to 1.8 degrees Celsius on average.[9]

However, climate change is more than global warming: it is defined as *"a significant variation of average weather conditions"*: becoming warmer, wetter, or drier—over decades or more.[10] There are also natural causes of climate variation such as volcanic eruptions, variation in solar radiation, the movement of crustal plates, and oscillation of the ocean and atmospheric system under El Nino–Southern Oscillation (ENSO),[11] however, it is anticipated that the frequency and severity of variations in weather patterns are increasing.

In this case, the longer-term trend differentiates climate change from natural weather variability.

Other impacts of human activity on the climate range from:

- Ambient temperature oscillations between hot and cold:
  - The most recent example is the extreme heat and long-term dry conditions that contributed to the unprecedented bushfires in Australia in 2019–2020. Bushfires burned through 46 million hectares (72,000 square miles).[12] There is no doubt that climate change is associated with the more frequent occurrence of bushfires: 2019 was the warmest year recorded since temperature recordings started.
  - Ice formation and heavy snowstorms.
- Landfill releasing methane and nitrous oxide as it breaks down.
- Increased precipitation from frequent and more intense rainfalls, leading to chemical-based weathering (carbonic acid that creates erosion along coastal regions and watercourses).
- Floods and high-water flow due to the expansion of human settlements and construction of infrastructure.
- Deforestation and the removal of carbon sinks via logging or clearcutting.

We need to appreciate that human civilization flourishes in a stable climate and that the planet is potentially accelerating toward instability based on the increased frequency and severity of extreme weather events. The socioeconomic impacts and hazards associated with extreme weather events are dramatic in terms of loss of human life, exemplified by the 2010 Russian heatwave that killed 55,000 people. Monetary losses of Hurricane Harvey equated to $125 billion (about $380 per person in the United States lost in 2017). As mentioned, climate change has worsened the hazards of extreme weather events; for instance, the Russian heatwave was estimated to be three times more likely due to global climate change.[13]

A global group of 11,000 scientists have endorsed 40 years of research on a range of measures that supports the hypothesis that the world is now facing a climate emergency; the research suggests that the following scenarios are plausible:[14]

- Twenty years from now, heavily populated parts of South Asia will more regularly face life-threatening heatwaves greater or equal to 34°C.
- The Sahara Desert will cross the Mediterranean Sea by 2030. This will mean that the heavily populated coast of Africa will be squeezed between the desert and the rising sea levels, impacting millions of people.
- Flammability of the Amazon will increase significantly based on a change in the fire season from 2021 to 2050 (using 1971–2000 as baseline for comparison).
- The coasts of China, Japan, and Korea will experience an increased frequency of what would have been rare rain events in the past, such as typhoons. Later in the century, systemic floods will present serious issues.

United Nations and Climate Change

Since 1992, the United Nations has been recognizing that changes to global climate patterns, and those at regional levels, pose serious issues to the world.[15] The recognition has created notable accords in negotiation with participating countries. Table 9.1 provides a summarized list of the talks and accords to date.

Scientific evidence on climate change and its impending impacts over the past 28 years has directed the accords. The Paris Agreement is no exception.

Table 9.1 History of United Nations Climate Accords

Year	United Nations talk and associated accords
1992	UN Framework Convention on Climate Change (UNFCCC)
1995	Berlin Mandate
1997	Kyoto Protocol
2001	Negotiations on the Kyoto Protocol that focused on emissions trading and how to account for carbon sinks in Bonn, Germany
2005	Kyoto Protocol takes effect excluding the United States
2007	Negotiations begin on Kyoto Protocol 2.0
2009	Copenhagen Accord
2010	Cancun Agreements
2011	Draft of a new legally binding agreement to take place in 2015. Extension of Kyoto 2.0 to 2017
2013	Warsaw International Mechanism for loss and damage with climate change impacts. Agreement also on initiative to end deforestation known as REDD+.
2015	Paris Agreement
2018	Rules for Paris Agreement decided
2019	UN Climate Action Summit for countries to submit nationally determined contribution plans as per the Paris Agreement
2020	Talks postponed due to the Covid19 pandemic. Emissions fall worldwide due to the pandemic, but reductions are not set to last.
2021	COP 26 Summit in Glasgow

In 2015, the Paris Agreement set a target for the net increase in global temperatures, to be limited to between 1.5 and 2 degrees Celsius. In general, there are two ways for participating countries to reach their agreed emissions targets. The first is to reduce emissions gradually over time, and the second, and more drastic approach, is to eliminate emissions by shutting down polluting facilities. The latter can be achieved by replacing fossil fuel production with renewable alternatives. Before we look at these options, let us look at the scientific reasons behind why emissions targets should be met.

Limitations of the Paris Accord Target

Even a temperature increase of less than 2 degrees Celsius will affect lives and livelihood: it will likely lead to flooding caused by an increase in frequency of extreme rainfall, an increase in sea levels, and an increased extent of wildfires. In addition, to meet the Paris targets, participating countries will need to make and sustain changes in industry sectors and energy usage to reduce emissions by at least 6% annually until 2030.[16] It has been reported that a new record in daily average carbon levels in the atmosphere was reached in 2021: it spiked to 421.21 parts per million, for the first time exceeding 420 parts per million. Such an increase, never before recorded in human history, confirmed that, according to sources, the planet's temperature increased by more than 2 degrees Celsius, compared to the Industrial Revolution.[17] Keep in mind, even if greenhouse gases were to reduce significantly overnight, the planet's temperature is expected to continue to increase due to the historical accumulation of CO_2 in the atmosphere.

Some research studies on climate change are suggesting that the Paris targets are not reasonably achievable, and that a 3 to 4 degrees Celsius warming is a more likely outcome.[18]

In its Fifth Assessment Report, the Intergovernmental Panel on Climate Change (IPCC) identified a set of representative concentration pathways (RCPs) that depict the greenhouse gas concentration (not emissions) trajectories under a range of warming scenarios.[19] Thus, RCP is a way to show how greenhouse gas concentration may develop over time. However, they do not account for the social and economic drivers. The Shared Socioeconomic Pathways (SSPs) were created to complete this picture.[20] Importantly, RCP and SSPs allow parallel approaches to better understand climate change scenarios, and the associated likely output warming. The IPCC has since published a Sixth Assessment Report that documents the individual contributions of three working groups focusing on physical sciences, climate change impacts (including adaptions and vulnerability), and mitigation. The report is a stock-take of current progress and provides the best- and worst-case scenarios of impacts on the environment and human society.[21]

INTERCONNECTED: CLIMATE AND FINANCIAL STABILITY

Following the Paris Agreement and COP26, there is broad awareness that transitioning to a low carbon economy poses significant risks, new challenges, but also investment opportunities for financial services. Several leading industry bodies provided well-defined guidance with global applicability such as:

- The Task Force on Climate-Related Disclosures (TCFD), formed by the Financial Stability Board to help companies understand what type of insights financial markets need on climate disclosures. At the time of writing, while TCFD disclosures are mandatory in the United Kingdom and New Zealand, over 3,000 organizations have joined and many are voluntarily reporting their climate-related disclosures.
- The Network for Greening the Financial System (NGFS), started by a group of Central Banks and supervisors in 2017, supporting the transition toward a sustainable economy creating and improving climate-related scenarios since 2020. The NGFS has, among other things, issued guidance on what is expected from central banks for disclosure and governance. The NGFS highlighted that the environment, the financial services industry, and customers are interconnected by a complex layer of interactions between the macroeconomic financial and climate systems.[22]
- The United Nations (UN) Environment Programme Finance Initiative developed a set of principles for the financial services industry, outlining responsibilities for climate change and climate-related risks.

The policy frameworks, guidelines, and principles are all supported by key assessments and reported data.

For organizations to effectively assess and address the risks associated with climate change, it is helpful to evaluate the channels by which climate change impacts the financial sector. These include:

Physical risk. Physical risk is the risk of physical damage caused by increased weather events such as hurricanes, floods, droughts, and heatwaves. As a region experiences more climate-related disruptions, there will also be indirect impacts on businesses through economic disruptions, potential supply-chain issues, and decline in values of commercial assets and homes.

Banks are already incorporating physical risk assessments of assets, and we explore the topic in more detail in the practical examples section.

Transition risk. Transition risks arise from transitioning to a lower-carbon economy. The major contributing factors are climate policies, consumer preferences, and carbon pricing.

Each of these climate risk categories transmits through the economy at both macroeconomic and microeconomic levels, to financial risks such as credit risk, market risk, liquidity risk, operational risk, and reputational risk.

ASSESSING THE IMPACTS OF CLIMATE CHANGE USING AI AND MACHINE LEARNING

For risk practitioners, to assess the impacts of climate change on portfolios and incorporate climate risk assessments in decision-making, questions about the accuracy and reliability of climate risk models prevail. The following considerations are highlighted:[23]

- There exists a large amount of uncertainty about the timing and magnitude of climate-based events.
- The nonlinear relationships between the macroeconomy and financial balance sheets are complex.
- There are direct and indirect influences of both physical and transition risks on the macroeconomy and financial balance sheets.
- There is additional complexity and interactions between physical and transition risks.

According to the Basel Committee, "A bank's ability to assess its overall exposure to climate risks across all of its significant operations will be heavily dependent upon the quality of its IT systems and its ability to aggregate and manage large amounts of data."

The above have influenced a growing amount of work[24,25] that suggests traditional models will not be adequate for modeling climate risk. Even if traditional approaches are used by risk modelers or climate scientists at least initially, these will require retuning or redevelopment at some stage. So, the larger question for risk managers becomes: "How do we use AI and machine learning to create accurate models that can reconstruct climate physical and transition risk drivers, retrain regularly, and capture the interconnections between the climate, the macroeconomy, and balance sheets?"

The scale and complexity of the climate change problem demand new thinking and new technologies, including the use of AI and machine learning. AI and machine learning are very effective at modeling complex relationships at scale, and that is exactly what is required in terms of climate risk. There are various auxiliary functions that are leveraging AI and machine learning to better assess and address climate change, including its use to better understand the extent of the problem, to monitor progress, and to address data quality issues.[26]

Firstly, analytics can help to better understand and define the climate risk problem. There is a lot of climate data available, like geospatial data, sensor data, and satellite images, but innovation is needed to analyze and combine it with traditional risk data and processes. New methods are needed to analyze new and unique types of data, including unstructured data (such as sentiment).

For example, with climate change it is well known that there is an increased risk of flooding—more frequent flooding will not only impact collateral values, but also supply chains and the long-term creditworthiness of a region. With the use of "smart city" analytics, sensors and rain gauges, residential areas can be better protected from flooding. By using newer technologies, monitoring water levels in real-time to predict flood risk, lives and livelihood can be better protected.

Secondly, to reduce greenhouse gas emissions, energy intensive and high-carbon industries will likely turn to buying carbon offsets. There are still open questions on how carbon offset markets are governed and how to guarantee the integrity of such a market, but computer vision and sensors can help monitor the greenhouse gas emissions of carbon offset projects.

And lastly, the use of AI and machine learning can assess data quality (see Chapter 2) and address data gaps through synthetic data creation.

But for now, we want to further explain the measures taken by the United Nations that have set targets to limit the rise of global temperatures to between 1.5 and 2 degrees Celsius, and how the most current targets are being used as the basis of climate risk scenarios for climate risk stress testing.

USING SCENARIO ANALYSIS TO UNDERSTAND POTENTIAL ECONOMIC IMPACTS

Financial institutions have started strengthening their climate risk assessment capacity. Now that the definition of climate risk is beginning to take shape, banks are in the planning stages of building the right governance frameworks.

Financial institutions will need well-considered environmental risk management expertise, but it is important that the banking industry develop their own capacity and not solely rely on regulators for guidance. Ideally, financial services industry will collaborate with regulators to further develop and refine regulations. There will also need to be local adjustments as each country has a unique set of social, economic, regional, and political conditions. Thus, the approaches to climate risk management will evolve over time.

For example, the Swedish regulator put a new policy in place: an aggressive target for its country to become the world's first net-zero fossil fuel emissions nation, as part of its Roadmap 2050.[27] Sweden has been on a *greening* journey to phase out its dependency on fossil fuels for over two decades. In addition, it has closed its last coal-fired power station two years ahead of schedule.[28] Adopting a similar approach of net-zero fossil-fuel emissions would simply be catastrophic in countries that rely heavily on fossil fuel. In this case, a disruptive, disorderly approach will likely have detrimental consequences:

- Energy cost increases could lead to significant increases in cost of electricity for households, business closures, and job losses.
- Significant supply chain issues would further drive an increase in the costs of goods and services.
- There are contagion effects on other downstream industries such as petrochemical plants that have infrastructure designed to derive chemical products.
- Living costs will increase.
- Inflation will increase.

This is not to say that complacency is welcome. Climate risk has a direct impact on the economic environment that the financial services industry operates in, their business operations, and counterparties. Organizations will need to be proactive and disciplined to make progress toward responding to climate risks. A fine balance between mitigating climate risk and ensuring financial stability will need to be established, which will be influenced by the vulnerabilities to climate risk and how it evolves, government policy responses, and customer expectations and needs. This is a journey!

Regulatory Guidance and Compliance Measures

In most cases, financial institutions are not waiting for governments to drive the large-scale action needed to mitigate financial risks. They are responding to signals from institutional investors (such as the IIGCC[29]) and the public to decarbonize their portfolios, announcing net-zero targets, and diversifying away from thermal coal lending.[30] In addition, they are creating sustainable finance and managing the financial and nonfinancial risks associated with climate instability.

Central banks and regulators are releasing forward-looking climate stress tests and disclosure expectations, mostly based on the recommendations by the Task Force on Climate-Related Financial Disclosures (TCFD).[31] The Financial Stability Board formed the TCFD to help companies understand what types of disclosures financial markets need on climate-related risks. Without this information, investors may incorrectly evaluate or price assets that can lead to a misallocation of capital. While this will support convergence and standardization, the climate stress tests and TCFD recommendations need calibration and adjustment by countries to be relevant in each jurisdiction.

To assess the impacts of climate change, many organizations are extending their scenario analysis and stress testing frameworks to include climate risk scenarios. This is also the approach adopted by many central banks. Scenario analysis is a helpful tool to, firstly, comply with climate-related regulatory stress testing and secondly, allow various stakeholders to better understand the shorter- and longer-term implications under a range of forward-looking scenarios, and plan accordingly.

Running climate-related stress tests is a good starting point. Keep in mind that, for financial institutions, in general, the narratives of regulatory stress testing may not be sufficient to capture the unique impacts of climate change. Regulatory stress tests rely on only a handful of scenarios and broad-brush model assumptions that are not necessarily specific to a firm's risk profile. Responses are heavily reliant on human judgment.

Although there are plans to make regulatory and industry scenarios more granular, the scenarios currently available do not capture the full range of potential pathways. In addition, these do not account for policy changes or mitigating actions: for example, mitigating events such as technological improvements in renewable energy to avoid the physical risks before financial losses are realized.[32]

In most cases, the stress testing models in use today do not account for propagation channels through micro- and macroeconomic drivers, nor the nonlinear relationships between risk factors, mostly due to the popular use of linear modeling techniques.[33]

In addition to facilitating a more granular level of analysis of complex, nonlinear relationships, i.e., help ascertain the direct and indirect influences of physical and transition risks on the micro- and macroeconomy, and subsequently on financial balance sheets, at the individual and interrelated level,[34] the use of AI and machine learning can help to better quantify the uncertainty of climate-based events.

Stress Testing: Getting a Foot in the Door

Once the fundamentals are in place, the simplest way for a bank to build their climate risk management capacity is to extend their stress testing framework to incorporate climate risk scenarios and simulations. The extension will require to run scenarios with much longer time horizons (to 2050 and even 2100). As mentioned earlier, regulators and other industry bodies are releasing forward-looking climate stress tests to help ease the burden on financial institutions having to design their own scenarios. Of these, the Bank of England's Prudential Regulatory Authority (PRA) has published one of the most comprehensive climate stress tests to date.[35] The developed 2021 biennial exploratory scenario (BES) has drawn from the lessons learned from climate scenarios in their 2019 Insurance Stress Tests. In addition, the NGFS has collaborated with climate scientists and published a set of climate scenarios. We will next describe both the BES and NGFS climate scenarios.

Biennial Exploratory Scenario

The Bank of England developed a 2021 biennial exploratory scenario (BES) that draws on the lessons learned from climate scenarios in the 2019 Insurance Stress Tests. The aim is to:

- Help understand the size of financial exposures of participating organizations to climate risk.
- Identify what the challenges are to models posed by climate risks.
- Help strengthen the management of climate risk of participating organizations and financial systems.

The key features of the BES are summarized in Figure 9.1 Key aspects include:

- Three scenarios, or stylized climate pathways, including physical and transition risk variables that are mapped to macroeconomic and financial variables.

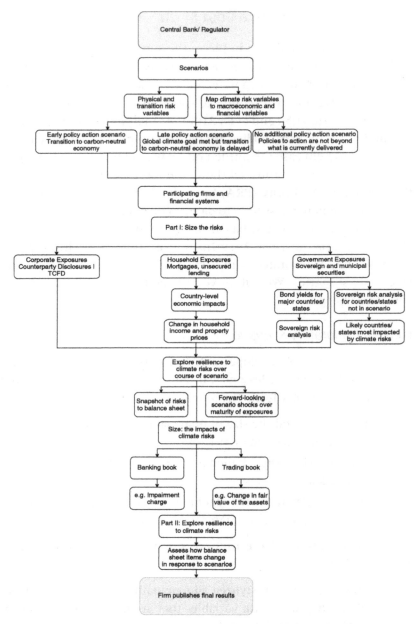

Figure 9.1 Key features of the Bank of England (BOE) biennial exploratory scenario (BES). Source: Adapted from Bank of England, 2019. Discussion Paper—The 2021 biennial exploratory scenario on the financial risks from climate change, London, United Kingdom: Bank of England.

- The scenarios include:
  1. Early policy action where transition to a carbon-neutral economy occurs early and a warming event of less than 2 degrees Celsius occurs in line with the Paris agreement
  2. Late policy action to align with global climate goals with a delay to transition to a carbon neutral economy
  3. No policy actions
- The climate risk variables include:
  - Physical risk variables
    - Global and regional temperature pathways
    - Frequency and severity of specific climate-related hazards in regions with material exposure (including UK flood, subsidence, and freeze)
    - Longevity
    - Agricultural productivity
  - Transition risk variables
    - Carbon price pathways
    - Emissions pathways (aggregate, and decomposed into regions and sectors)
    - Commodity and energy prices (including renewables), by fuel type
    - Energy mix
  - The corresponding macroeconomic and financial variables include:
    - Macroeconomic variables
    - Real GDP (gross domestic product)—aggregate and decomposed by sector
    - Unemployment rate
    - Inflation
    - Central bank rates

- Corporate profits—aggregate and decomposed by sector
- Household income
- Residential and commercial property prices
- Financial variables
  - Government bond yields for major economies
  - Corporate bond yields for major economies—investment grade and high yield
  - Equity indices
  - Exchange rates
  - Bank rates

As part of sizing the risks on their assets of the climate scenarios, participants modeled the impact based on three levels of granularity, namely: corporate exposures, household exposures, and government exposures. For these exposures, participants were encouraged to assess individual corporate counterparty-risk using climate disclosures like those released by the TCFD. A challenge was how to assess corporate counterparties at the counterparty level, given that there is not a standardized set of information on emissions data available. The regulator used the findings from the exploratory exercise to assess the safety and soundness of the financial system under the different scenarios, and to determine whether additional capital to absorb climate risk losses is necessary. Based on the responses from participants and the analysis of the regulator, a key finding from the CBES exercise is that climate risk will place a drag on the profitability of banks, making the system more vulnerable to future potential shocks. At this stage, the regulator did not introduce a climate-specific capital add-on.[36]

Climate Scenarios Developed by the Network for Greening the Financial System

The Network for Greening the Financial System (NGFS) published climate scenarios in 2020 and their updated version in 2021. A set of six scenarios were provided based on these dimensions:

- **Orderly scenarios.** Climate risk policies are introduced early and become more stringent over time.
- **Disorderly scenarios.** Climate risk policies are either delayed or vary across countries and sectors.
- **Hothouse scenarios.** Climate risk policies are implemented in some jurisdictions only, but overall global efforts are insufficient to address climate change.

Despite the challenges associated with climate stress testing, scenario analysis and simulations, and heavy reliance on expert judgment, several financial institutions in jurisdictions such as those across Europe, the Middle East, and Africa (EMEA) and Asia Pacific (APAC) are building capacity to improve quantifying climate risk by collecting climate data, integrating that with their incumbent data management processes, and performing early-stage stress testing and scenario analysis that are broadly aligned to those of the NGFS. Financial institutions are either utilizing their existing risk models by augmenting with climate-based variables, or creating new climate risk models.

Firms Can Start by Strengthening Their Analytics Frameworks

With all this in mind, it is no wonder that organizations are not sure where to start.

Although most central banks have issued guidelines on how regulated entities, including banks, can apply prudent practices for climate risk management, in many jurisdictions a lack of clarity remains on:

- The key data and parameter requirements for different stress testing scenarios
- Endorsement of credible and commonly used scenarios apart from those provided by the NGFS
- Details on how institutions should conduct short- and long-term scenario analysis

To not be caught off guard, for organizations a good starting point is to review their capability to see if it meets the fundamentals of a robust analytic ecosystem (Figure 9.2):

1. Data sourcing and its management, including data validation and quality assurance.

2. A risk-modeling platform for data-derived insights leveraging quantitative techniques and procedures.

3. Risk calculations and simulation capability.

4. Integration with impact assessments, business decision-making, and reporting.

Organizations will need granular physical and transition risk data, and that data will require use of advanced data-quality procedures to assure data quality. High-performance, parallel-processing engines can accommodate the granular data requirements and frequency of forward-looking risk simulation cycles.

As we know, data is the foundation of any analytics-derived outcome. Without the quality, validation, and assurance measures of data, the outcome is likely to be inferior. Provided that climate risk modeling is a relatively new topic, climate risk data for measuring financial impacts is not that readily available, especially loan-level information, and not yet of adequate quality to support large-scale, robust model development and simulation.

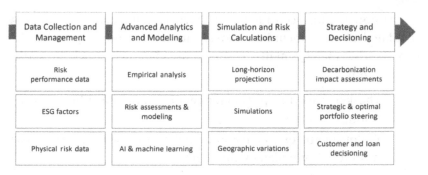

Figure 9.2 A proposed framework to create a climate risk ecosystem.

To better address the limitations, organizations will need to focus on the following areas to achieve robustness in their climate risk management efforts:

- Ensure data quality:
  - Establish a robust data-quality framework consistent with BCBS (Basel Committee on Bank Supervision) 239 principles for internal and third-party climate-related data.
  - Supply full transparency, such as source of the data, methods used to transform variables, and geospatial level of granularity.
- Expand scenario coverage:
  - Strengthen scenario analysis capability.
  - Streamline the management of multiple scenarios.
  - Incorporate flexibility for portfolio growth to reflect business strategy and run-off assumptions.
  - Quickly and efficiently meet the expanding challenges of supervisory stress testing to include longer time horizons and expanded risk factors.
  - Expand capabilities to support scenario-based business planning.
- Improve modeling:
  - Put in place a more sophisticated modeling environment that can be used to develop models for physical and transition risk, to also enrich models such as those used for expected credit losses (ECL) and risk-weighted assets (RWA).
  - Ensure that the modeling environment can be extended to include modern AI and machine learning models.
- Improve process efficiency:
  - Accelerate model implementation through a more simplified model deployment mechanism for adjustment and recalibration.
    - Automate manual processes and the documentation of adjustments and overrides of analytic-derived outcomes.

▪ Increase collaboration.

  ▪ Centrally orchestrate the entire climate risk management process.
  ▪ Ensure consistency processes across the enterprise.
  ▪ Ensure climate risk forms part of the enterprise risk governance framework and is integrated with existing risk systems.

PRACTICAL EXAMPLES

AI and machine learning are very effective at modeling complex relationships at scale and that is exactly what is required in terms of climate risk. The broad set of applications of AI and machine learning makes it particularly effective as a tool in the fight against climate change. Included in this section are a few tangible examples where AI and machine learning are effectively employed to assist climate risk management.

With the increased adoption of cloud-based computing, an example of that is a cloud computing providers, namely Google, who initiated the development of a machine learning application, called Deepmind, to improve energy efficiency in the cooling of their data centers. The Deepmind project employs ensembles of neural networks to predict energy efficiency. The models capture the dynamic interactions between the temperature observed from sensors, power pump speeds, and other parameters within their data centers. The project led to a significant reduction in energy consumption of 40%.[37]

Another example is in the increased risk of flooding. The increased risk of flooding is a major physical risk due the increased risk of natural disasters. Physical hazards, such as flooding, have potential to impact not only the collateral values associated with banks' exposures, but also the cost of capital and affordability of insurance. It can have a knock-on impact on businesses, supply chains, and the long-term creditworthiness of a region. Recently, an American town planner employed AI and machine learning on a smart city project to better protect residents from river flooding. By installing sensors and rain gauges to monitor water levels in real-time and using that data and analytics to predict flood risk, residents can be warned proactively and traffic is rerouted. In this case, the use of

AI and real-time data mitigates the socioeconomic impacts of the increased risk of flooding.

Climate Risk Management Solution

Recognizing the need for an enterprise climate risk solution, a Tier 1 bank in Asia Pacific extended their stress testing solution to quantify the impacts of climate risk following a bottom-up analytical approach. They employed scenario analysis with supporting internal and external reports. A climate risk model assesses the impacts of each industry or subindustry's decline in asset values and quantifies the climate risk at exposure level. It links the bank's portfolio strategy with its finance and auditing processes for business planning and policy decision-making.

Environmental, Social, and Governance Application in APAC-Based Financial Companies

For financial institutions, assessing the carbon emissions of counterparties presents practical challenges in data collection. In this case, the firm employed AI and machine learning to upload and process sustainability reports and counterparty information on a cloud-based platform. Geo-location data, scenario, and other risk data from third-party providers are uploaded through APIs. By modeling the real estate data, disaster prediction data, and financial data of the counterparty, the degree of financial impact and the impact on collateral value are projected. The information is then used to assess the impacts of climate risk on the counterparty's balance sheet and P&L.

Sustainability Investment Screening

An analytics company in the Nordics created a sustainability investment screening solution to help their clients. By utilizing its web interface, financial investors can select companies that are more sustainable than others. The solution performs investment screening and monitoring based on the use of unstructured data, machine learning algorithms, and an intelligent triage process.

Specifically, the solution incorporates the corporate entities of existing investments. The application downloads the annual reports of each company that the client's financial investors are considering for investing, via the Danish registry, in the form of unstructured textual information. In addition, it uses sustainability reports from the UN Global Database via Robotic Process Automation (RPA). In this case, RPA was needed because an API was unavailable. The RPA performs screen-scraping, extracts the information, and stores it in a structured dataset. The sustainability reports include sustainability development goals (SDGs), as well as human rights, labor rights, the environment, and anti-corruption information.

AI and machine learning are used to improve the process by identifying climate-specific information using new types of data, generating SDG scores, and analyzing trends and variations.

CONCLUDING REMARKS

For financial institutions, there is a pressing need to incorporate climate risk in their financial decision-making and risk management processes. As we find ourselves in the decisive decade with regards to transitioning to a lower carbon economy, there is an urgency for financial institutions to lead the way in sustainable finance and help manage both the financial and nonfinancial risks of the transition. The scale and complexity of the problem demand new thinking and new technologies. With that in mind, it's imperative for organizations to build their climate risk management capacity early: in forward-looking climate risk modeling approaches and employing AI and machine learning responsibly.

ENDNOTES

1. Mark Carney, *Breaking the Tragedy of the Horizon—Climate Change and Financial Stability* (London: Bank of England, 2015).
2. NGFS, *NGFS: Central Banks and Supervisors Network for Greening the Financial System* (2019) https://www.ngfs.net/en
3. NASA, *Scientific consensus: Earth's climate is warming* (2021) https://climate.nasa.gov/scientific-consensus/
4. CDC, *Air Quality* (2021) https://www.cdc.gov/air/pollutants.htm

5. Thomas F. Stocker, Qin Dahe, Gian-Kasper Plattner, M. Tignor, et al. *IPCC. Climate Change 2013: The Physical Science Basis. Contribution of Working Group I to the Fifth Assessment Report of the Intergovernmental Panel on Climate Change* (Cambridge, United Kingdom and New York: Cambridge University Press, 2013).

6. J. Kelly, *The Top 10 Causes of Global Warming* (Santa Monica, CA: Leaf Group Ltd., 2019).

7. Melissa Denchak, *Global Climate Change: What You Need to Know* (New York: NRDC, 2017).

8. Denchak, *Global Climate Change: What You Need to Know.*

9. AZoCleantech, *The Connection Between Waste Management & Global Warming* (Manchester, United Kingdom: AZoCleantech, 2008).

10. Denchak, *Global Climate Change: What You Need to Know.*

11. Climate Science Investigations, *Causes of Climate Change—Natural Causes of Climate Change* (Washington, DC: NASA, 2016).

12. Tahnee Burgess, James R. Burgmann, Stephanie Hall, David Holmes, and Elizabeth Turner, Burgess, T. et al., *Black Summer—Australian Newspaper Reporting of the Nation's Worst Bushfire Crisis* (Melbourne, Australia: Monash Climate Change Communication Research Hub, Monash University. 2020), https://www.monash.edu/__data/assets/pdf_file/0009/2121111/Black-Summer-Australian-newspaper-reporting-of-the-nations-worst-bushfire-season.pdf

13. Christopher R. Schwalm, *Forecasting Climate Change Risk: A Ticking Time Bomb* (Woods Hole, Falmouth, MA: Woodwell Climate Research Center, 2021).

14. William J. Ripple, et al., "World Scientists' Warning of a Climate Emergency," *BioScience* 70(1) (2020): 8–12; Schwalm, *Forecasting Climate Change Risk.*

15. Basel Committee on Banking Supervision, *Climate-related risk drivers and their transmission channels* (Basel, Switzerland: Bank for International Standards (BIS), 2021).

16. Anastasios Petropoulos, Vasilis Siakoulis, Nikolaos Vlachogiannakis, and Evaggelos Stavroulakis, *Deep-Stress: A Deep Learning Approach for Dynamic Balance Sheet Stress Testing* (Paris, France: European Banking Authority (EBA), 2019).

17. Alla Gil, *How to Stress Test for Extremely Unexpected Scenarios* (New Jersey, NY: Global Association of Risk Professionals (GARP), 2021).

18. Climate change AI, 2022, https://www.climatechange.ai/

19. The United Nations, *UN Climate Talks 1992–2020* (New York City: The United Nations, 2020).

20. William McDonnell, *The Heat Is on: Insurability and Resilience in a Changing Climate* (Amsterdam, The Netherlands: CRO Forum, 2019); Matthew Cappucci and Jason Samenow, *Carbon dioxide spikes to critical record, halfway to doubling preindustrial levels* (Washington, DC: Washington Post, 2021).

21. Cappucci and Samenow, Carbon dioxide spikes to critical record.

22. Climate Action Tracker. *Climate Action Tracker—Find your country* (2021) https://climateactiontracker.org/countries

23. Rajendra K. Pachauri and Leo Meyer, *Climate Change 2014: Synthesis Report. Contribution of Working Groups I, II and III to the Fifth Assessment Report of the Intergovernmental Panel on Climate Change* (Geneva, Switzerland: IPCC, 2014).

24. McDonnell, 2019, *The Heat Is on.*

25. IPCC, *Sixth Assessment Report* (Geneva, Switzerland, 2022), https://www.ipcc.ch/assessment-report/ar6/; McDonnell, *The Heat Is on*.

26. NGFS, *NGFS—Central Banks and Supervisors Network for Greening the Financial System*.

27. Jonas Allerup, *Sweden's Climate Act and Climate Policy Framework* (Stockholm, Sweden: Swedish Environmental Protection Agency, 2020).

28. Frédéric Simon, *Sweden Adds Name to Growing List of Coal-Free States in Europe* (Brussels, Belgium: Euractive, 2020).

29. Net zero investment framework implementation guide, IIGCC (April 13, 2021), https://www.iigcc.org/resource/net-zero-investment-framework-implementation-guide/

30. Charlotte Grieve, *Big Four Banks Forced to Defend Thermal Coal Exit* (Melbourne, Australia: The Age, 2021).

31. Task Force on Climate-related Financial Disclosures, *TCFD—Task Force on Climate-related Financial Disclosures* (2020), https://www.fsb-tcfd.org/

32. Sharon Thiruchelvam, *Does regulators' favourite climate risk metric measure up?* (Risk .net publication, 2021), https://www.risk.net/regulation/7899226/does-regulators-favourite-climate-risk-metric-measure-up.

33. Petropoulos et al., *Deep-Stress*.

34. Petropoulos et al., *Deep-Stress*.

35. Bank of England, *Discussion Paper—The 2021 Biennial Exploratory Scenario on the Financial Risks from Climate Change* (London: Bank of England, 2019).

36. Bank of England, *Results of the climate biennial exploratory scenario* (May 24, 2022), https://www.bankofengland.co.uk/stress-testing/2022/results-of-the-2021-climate-biennial-exploratory-scenario

37. Richard Evans and Jim Gao, *DeepMind AI Reduces Google Data Centre Cooling Bill by 40%* (July 20, 2016), https://www.deepmind.com/blog/deepmind-ai-reduces-google-data-centre-cooling-bill-by-40

About the Authors

Terisa Roberts is a director and Global Solution lead for Risk Modeling and Decisioning at SAS. She has extensive experience in quantitative risk management, regulatory compliance, and model governance and validation. She has worked in financial services, telecommunications, government, energy, and retail sectors.

She advises banks and regulators around the world on best practices in risk modeling and decisioning and the responsible use of artificial intelligence and machine learning. She regularly speaks at international conferences on the application of innovative models in risk management.

She holds a PhD in Operations Research and Informatics and lives in Sydney, Australia, with her family.

Stephen J. Tonna is a senior banking solutions advisor at SAS. He is a PhD-trained professional with 10 years of statistical, scientific, and industry experience.

The passion to discover practical ways to use artificial intelligence and associated methodologies like machine learning and deep learning as transformation tools is one reason that gets him up in the morning!

At SAS, Stephen advises with specialized expertise in risk in the main areas of credit scoring and decisioning, model risk management, and how these and many other offerings can be used to realize risk transformation in the cloud.

He thoroughly enjoys complex change management projects and finds it exciting to instill thought leadership to effect digital change and discover unrealized areas of process improvement.

Stephen lives in Melbourne, Australia, with his wife, Nini, and son, Sebastian James.

Index

Page numbers followed by *f* and *t* refer to figures and tables, respectively.